UNIVERSAL SYMBOLS

Keys to Your Consciousness

KEN DOWLING

Universal Symbols

Copyright © 2012 by Ken Dowling

All rights reserved. No part of this book may be used or reproduced by any means, graphic, electronic, or mechanical, including photocopying, recording, taping or by any information storage retrieval system without the written permission of the publisher except in the case of brief quotations embodied in critical articles and reviews.

This Universal Symbols book may be ordered online through:
www.universalsymbols.com.au

ISBN: 978-0-646-58828-5

Because of the dynamic nature of the Internet, any web addresses or links contained in this book may have changed since publication and may no longer be valid. The views expressed in this work are solely those of the author and do not necessarily reflect the views of the publisher, and the publisher hereby disclaims any responsibility for them.

The author of this book does not dispense medical advice or prescribe the use of any technique as a form of treatment for physical, emotional, or medical problems without the advice of a physician, either directly or indirectly. The intent of the author is only to offer information of a general nature to help you in your quest for emotional and spiritual well–being. In the event you use any of the information in this book for yourself, which is your constitutional right, the author and the publisher assume no responsibility for your actions.

The Cover Design and Digital Artwork for the Symbols
by Morgan Dowling of mdsign.com.au.
www.universalsymbols.com.au
Facebook/Universal Symbols

Printed in Australia.

CONTENTS

Dedication vii
Preface ix
Introduction xv

My Story 1
Knowing Spirit 8
Spiritual Healing 13
Background of the Symbols .19
Working with the Symbols 25
The Symbols 30
New Beginning 247
About the Author 251
Index of Symbols 253

DEDICATION

The inspiration for this creation is my beautiful spirit and the wonderful wisdom shared so willingly with me by my many guides, healers, teachers and friends. I feel that all of my life has led me to this realisation, all pieces of the puzzle coming together serendipitously to create this magical kaleidoscope I call my life. One day you wake up feeling totally different and at peace with your uniqueness. This is your day to be free. We have all been through so much to understand and live our lives with real meaning. When you acknowledge your intuitive energetic spirit, you will know all you need to know exactly when you need to. I am truly grateful for all my experiences, mostly self created or at least co-created with other souls sharing my karmic journey. We have been guided, inspired, loved and shared in many ways and I pray that you are finding your loving way.

To my long departed parents wherever you may be, travel well Issy and Tedley. Thank you for my life, for your love and all the guidance you have provided me in this life and from beyond. You have been a tower of strength and wisdom particularly when I have lost my way or forgotten who I really was. I know that you and all the angels, guides, teachers, healers and masters have watched over and guided me tirelessly when I have neglected or mistaken my life's path. I know that spirit is always with me, is always within me and omnipresent in all of my life. If ever a soul could choose to do it the hard way, then I will accept the stubborn, obstinate approach is not the softer of the options.

For everyone who has ever shared my love, thank you for your love, patience, perseverance and tolerance. I know that it is not always easy to live with or love a sensitive, strong willed and powerful soul who may not have always remembered who he was meant to be. I accept that all of my life, every one of my experiences has delivered me to this moment and for that I am truly grateful. My children, Flynn, Morgan and Jasmine, you are my inspiration, my realisation and my love. You are all very special in your own unique ways. I pray you have received your solid foundation for life and you are free to fully explore all life's magical possibilities. Be lovingly honest with yourselves and life will be true to you. I am extremely grateful to Morgan for designing the wonderful cover and digitalising the symbols for this book.

Kylie, you are my wonderful partner in life and in love. What a journey we have shared. You are truly beautiful, loving, generous, caring, energetic, wise and the gentlest soul I could wish to be with. Without your support, assistance and gentle persuasion, much of my gift would still be within me. We enjoy this evolutionary journey together, exploring our love and all the magic of our universal energy. May we continue to be truly blessed, connected and live our lives with complete love and honour. Thank you.

PREFACE

The key strength of symbology is in their ability to communicate directly with your soul. When you consider most of the significant images, messages or signposts in your life, they will be of a symbolic nature. Symbols are very powerful and effective tools to simply convey universal messages, intention or meaning. From ancient civilisations right through to this day, symbols have been used for tribal markings, inscriptions and totems to corporate logos, road signage, brands, technological and religious icons. Since the dawn of time, we have communicated symbolically with sound, colour, pictures, common words or meanings. Generally we seem to accept and adopt these concepts or images into our psychic and vocabulary relatively quickly and painlessly. On the other hand, energetic or spiritual symbols have always been regarded somewhat with suspicion and scepticism. Too often they have been misused, misinterpreted or demonised by misguided souls in positions of power and control. Unfortunately it is not the symbols that cause harm. Human beings hold this monopoly. Symbols are simply an effective tool of invoking conscious intention. They are one of the many universal gifts we have been provided to understand and comprehend more of ourselves and our spiritual essence.

During his search for greater meaning and purpose in his life, the author, Ken Dowling has channelled over 500 unique Universal Symbols. These energetic symbols are original and here to assist humanity to shift our consciousness in this the 21st century. Ken has intimate knowledge of each of his symbols, having worked on himself and thousands of clients in Australia over the last 11 years. Each of these symbols represents an individual key to our consciousness, unlocking the infinite energy, memory and potential of the soul. The real power of the symbols lies in their ability to by-pass any intellectual fixations or emotional blockages held with the psychic body to release, energise and amplify the individual's evolutionary journey. Souls who have integrated these symbols into their lives have reported significant positive changes in many aspects of their lives. All positive and lasting change can only be initiated by your-self and when you are ready, the guidance and tools you need will be presented to you.

As a species we have never been more challenged in how we are living together on this beautiful and resourceful planet. For as long as humans have ignored their spiritual essence, there has been perpetual conflict between nations, religions, cultures and each other. We have such an insatiable thirst for material wealth, power and excess while poverty, famine, isolation, loneliness and environmental degradation prevail all around us. Everywhere you look there is social dysfunction, unhappiness, negativity, fear, sickness, depression, separation, emptiness, suffering and despair. We have been programmed to believe that when we have more than we could ever physically need or use in a thousand lifetimes, we will be able to live the way that we really desire. Yet we are all still striving and grasping to attain some resemblance of happiness and meaning, surrounded by the trappings of intellectualism, material wealth and physical achievement. It is only when you have possessed everything that you thought you had ever wanted that you will find that you really have very little at all. In this obsessive struggle for physical success, we have lost our connection to our soul's energy and its purpose for this incarnation.

This was Ken's experience after investing 25 years of his life in the corporate world. He had achieved far more than he ever imagined he would, however he did not like himself much or enjoy the view when he arrived at the summit of his career. In the process of climbing the corporate ladder, he had compromised himself, his values and everything he had treasured at that time. After having his career effectively terminated, he left his job highly disenchanted, totally exhausted and disillusioned. This catalyst instigated his search for real meaning and purpose in his life. He read everything he could lay his hands on, studied a wide range of belief systems, attended many seminars and courses on metaphysics, undertook spiritual healings and counselling, trained and shared with many wise souls and friends.

His search for greater wisdom led him to Reiki (Universal Energy). He learnt Reiki purely to help understand his own spiritual nature and to heal his own wounds at the time. Reiki had a profound impact on his life through providing the keys to open the door to his soul. Walking through this doorway, opening to deeper aspects of his soul memory ultimately triggered his access to an infinite range of symbols that are held within the Universal Akashic Records. While reluctant and even sceptical at first to use these symbols, Ken spent considerable time in meditation working with the symbols inside him-self to reveal aspects and qualities he had previously not experienced. Having just come from the intellectual, rational corporate world, it was a struggle to let go of his rigid logic to allow the energy of these symbols to weave their magical powers. His evidence within himself was overwhelming, each symbol he received had unique energy, unlocked hidden potential and gifts, removed blockages and fears, activated and accelerated desired energies and aspirations. Once he accepted that he was actually healing and growing through this revelation and working with the symbols, he realised the real power of the gift he had to share.

Using these symbols is quite simple, painless and cannot harm you contrary to popular opinion. Symbols are not the work of demons or dishonourable, unloving souls. Every symbol has been brought into existence with pure loving intention, activated to contribute towards our collective evolution in a real positive and loving way. These symbols cannot be misused, abused or cause you harm. Should anyone desire to use the symbols with negative intent, the only being they will affect will be themselves. The symbols will accelerate and amplify any human negativity and fear to enable the soul to reveal its true loving, positive nature. It is true that people do hurt people, we all see this every day. However this is still the main play on this physical plane where we are still experiencing who we are not. Look deeper into your pain and suffering and you will find your soul connection and your karma. This is where your healing begins and your suffering will end.

The symbols do not require belief or even faith to be effective. Just surrender and allow your-self to experience the energy of the symbols. Initially you may not feel a great deal or experience any real shift in your perspective. Just remember that you have not attuned your-self to this or any energy for some time and it will take time and practice for you to assimilate your-self with this unique energy. The symbols amplify and accelerate your own intention enabling you to create more or less of particular energies or experiences in your life. Depending on where your intention and focus is directed, you will achieve the spiritual outcome you desire. It is important to remember that your physical energy will always follow your spirit's intention whether you are aware of this or not. Your focussed intention is your creative power.

The symbol for Spirit was the first symbol that Ken received in 2001 and this symbol was confirmed later in a book he had ordered months earlier. The symbol for Spirit or the Sun appears in most cultures on the planet with a similar meaning or intention. Many of the symbols he has channelled have been recognised and inspired by many cultures including Aboriginal, Maori, Egyptian, Tibetan, Indian, Celt, Druid, Aztec, Star Being, Lemurian and Atlantean. Ken does not profess to be an expert on symbology or their origins nor has he conducted comprehensive research or analysis of their human history. He has simply worked with and experienced the energy within himself to know their impact and effectiveness in transmuting negativity and fearful programs within the energy field of his body. His knowing has been developed from his experiences within himself and with thousands of his customers.

This book features over 100 of his symbols, each with its own energy, intention and meaning. It is designed to help people to be able to help themselves either by reading the book in its entirety or by randomly opening a page for its particular guidance. Each page has been written to stand alone with sufficient explanation available for the reader to be able to take action to effect real change in their own lives. These symbols work on many levels, whether it is spiritual, emotional, physical, energetic, sensory and psychological. The symbols release and unlock any residual energy within the soul to increase and enhance the consciousness of the reader. This healing process is very individual and requires every being to be totally responsible for everything they feel, think, express and do. Being responsible for your-self can be challenging and very rewarding as you have regained your power.

Every soul who is attracted to these symbols will experience significant changes in their lives. You cannot change one aspect of your-self without affecting other parts of you or others. All energy is in constant movement and you will not be able to change and remain the same. You may not necessarily change what you are doing, however you will change how you are in the doing. It is important to be aware of how your energy is shifting and be conscious of the impact you may have on others. Take care to be loving and compassionate with your-self or others to ensure you do not develop any further negative karma or energetic bondage. Your change is your change, just as your life is your life. It is not necessary for anyone else to change with you in the same way. Remember that your soul is always loving, positive, simple and honourable. Be who you are and who you have always meant to be and you will experience your special life of spirit. Enjoy your journey and be your love.

INTRODUCTION

I graciously welcome you with many blessings of joyous love. You are a very special being of the light, living and evolving during these extraordinary times. All that has come before you, every experience and event in your life has led you right to this moment in your awareness. You have the opportunity and ability to create the life you have always dreamed of and by doing so, you will be able to positively influence the quality of all life. All human experience, celebration, achievement, turmoil, conflict and change stimulates our spiritual evolution throughout the universe. We all have a unique role to play and you will rediscover your purpose when you remember all of who you really are.

It is time for you to realise and release your full spiritual potential. Reconnect with your soul essence to provide the energy and guidance to illuminate your path. All matter in existence is soul energy all vibrating to serve its evolutionary purpose in the greater body of the universe. You are a vital soul element within this universal body with your distinct and important part to play. There is no separation, there is no disconnection, there is no in here or out there. We are all together in the one body of all existence. When you realise that you are not alone, that no-one energetically fits in these physical life forms and that everyone feels similarly to your-self, you will begin to realise that only you can make a real difference in your own life. Change can only begin from within your-self and this is your soul responsibility. You are the source and soul experience of your energy. It is now time for you to fully embrace you.

Not everyone is ready to accept their true nature. Humanity seems to prefer the long suffering struggle and the familiarity of stress, depression and sadness. Drama and trauma have always been with us to highlight the imbalances between the light and dark, positive and negative, love and fear based energies we utilise to feed our evolution. We have all experienced our fair share of dramatic growth and despair and it is only when you realise that you deserve better, that you will make new positive choices. Every experience we have is a direct result of our own choices. Your current life style is an accumulation of your choices to this point, where you find your-self now is a choice, in every moment you are making choices whether you are conscious or not. Each and every choice you make is a highly creative process initiated solely by your-self. It is only when you take full responsibility for your soul's creation that you will become more aware of your choices. More importantly, you will become fully aware of your primary motivation driving these choices. When you accept that there is more to your life than just your physicality, you will know that you are fully connected to and part of the infinite energy of the universe.

There are no chance happenings or accidents in evolution. Every incident, every event, every moment has purposeful intention and meaning. Some of us would like to dismiss away these events by believing they just happen or are created by others when in effect nothing occurs in your life that is not here for you to learn from. There are wise beings amongst us who learn exceptionally well from both their positive and negative experiences, making the most of their opportunities and always acting upon their spiritual guidance. These are the souls to emulate and to learn from, seek them out and strive to be the best you can be. If you find your-self still learning negatively and fearfully from the drama, the suffering, the searching, the grasping and from the illusion of physical life, then find a different, more positive and loving way of dealing with these situations. Consider for a moment, when you continually recreate the same experience of life, you always remain the same and nothing will change. When you desire to be different, changes will present in your life and it will be your responsibility to make more conscious choices to sustain your new life.

The energy you are about to encounter here is a reflection of my story and my experience of changing my life. It is interesting when you set your intention to change even in some small way that nothing is left out of this process. You will not only look within your-self, you will test all your relationships, attachments, beliefs, habits, rituals, stories, possessions, wounds and illusions. No stone will be left unturned nor will any of your issues be unaddressed in your commitment to fully understand and accept all of your-self. There will be times when you question your sanity and the reality of what you have undertaken. Have the faith and courage within your-self that you are on your path and you will become clearer and more loving along your way. Time is a great healing teacher. Everything will present itself to you when you are ready to receive. With sufficient time and space, you will see and feel life in your own way and you will be okay. Be sure to be as loving to your-self and others as you can be for this is the energy you are seeking to be.

Enjoy your journey with my gift. These words are the result of my journey; they are my truth and reflect how I strive to live my love. Sometimes I am more successful than others, however I do now know who I am and I am blessed to truly love all of my-self and this is the love I endeavour to share with you.

Allow your-self to relax, take your time and surrender to the energy you are about to encounter, for these symbols will shift your energy and focus in this life. It is important that you become more aware of your-self and your inner feelings while you are reading this material for you will be changing and shifting your energy all the time. The symbols are very powerful and effective in transmuting and converting all fearful, negative energies into positive, loving energy within your-self and all around you. The impact of the symbols' energy will remain with you for some time and you may feel the effect of what you have read for weeks after your experience of it. Do not be alarmed or fearful for this process is necessary. You will not clear your-self with one reading, healing or treatment, all change takes time and it will take some time for you to adjust to the new you that you are creating. Remember that you cannot change and remain the same. Be a little patient and kind to your-self in the process. Positive, loving change always nurtures your soul. Be sure to love your-self totally through your evolution and this will be the energy you create all around you.

MY STORY

All the symbols contained in this book were inspired and channelled during my spiritual journey. In the year 2000, the symbols started to come to me from many spiritual sources, guides and spiritual teachers during meditations, while creating my art or randomly in my consciousness at the oddest times. It may sound incredulous but I had been drawing these shapes and patterns for most of my life and really thought nothing of it. Having a traditional work background in the logical, seemingly rational corporate world, letting go of intellectual control to embark on spiritual energy work was never in the realms of consideration.

Early in the 90s, I was working incredibly hard, studying for my Masters in Business Administration (MBA) with three children under four years old and I knew something had to give. At the time, I remember commenting to a colleague that I felt like I was strapped into a out of control race car having severed the brake lines myself and I knew that there was a wall at the end of the straight that I was going to hit, hard and fast. It took another six years to hit this wall and this I did well. In 1997, feeling very disconnected and disillusioned, I had a premonition that if I did not change the way I was living, that I would be dead within ten years. On a sub-conscious level, I did not want this outcome and with just this one thought, my whole life imploded within the next 12 months. There was not an aspect of my life that did not shift dramatically. I changed my life in every way and these changes made wide ranging and lasting impacts on my-self and everyone around me. This was a totally surreal and extremely challenging time in my life. One that I would never have thought I'd ever have the courage to face or have the strength to find my way through. At the time it felt like I was passing from one lifetime to another without actually leaving this body and this tested my resolve in every way.

With hindsight, I possibly could have handled things differently and more lovingly, however I was typically bull headed and too self possessed to procrastinate any longer. It is hard to imagine now, but at the time it felt like life or death, as melodramatic as that may sound. Questioning everything you know to be true is not an easy or safe road to travel. You will test your-self to your essence to try to make some sense of this life. Most of us hide within the confines of what we know and feel comfortable within and this was certainly true for me. I was numb to life, going through the paces, doing what I thought was required of me and I felt empty, unfulfilled and totally alone. I knew that I was not happy with my relationship, my work and my life. I also knew exactly what the costs and consequences would be when I finally found the courage to make new choices with my life. It was going to cost me everyone and everything I cherished and it very nearly did. When you find your-self seeking dramatic alternatives, even death to escape your existence, then it is time to take stock and to make decisions that honour your soul's journey. Most of us are not really living. We just exist within our malaise from day to day, killing ourselves slowly with our unsustainable, unhealthy and self abusive life styles. This was my life.

It is difficult to know after an event if things could have been different, however we all create and make choices every day that shape and alter our paths. Being comfortably numb to life is not excusable and conservatively playing it safe only confines us to the shackles of our meagre existence. This is not living or being alive to the unique possibilities life and love has to offer you. I am not suggesting that you make radical or dramatic changes in your life. Although you should identify what is really important to you and examine ways of improving the quality of your life experience. Your best life is not about the acquisition of more possessions, money or power, these temporary physical attributes are far less important than the integrity of your soul. Changing the quality of your life is about you feeling really alive again, excited about all of life and being interested in being here to fulfil your purpose. Now that has some merit and is worth pursuing, don't you feel?

You know that there are few spirits in this human form that really feel that they fit on this earth plane and most kill or destroy any real sense of themselves in the process of trying so bloody hard to fit. If you feel like you are a horse in a herd of sheep there is a good reason for that, you quite possibly are. Every soul in existence has its unique journey. We are shaped by our experiences, acquiring gifts and skills through many lifetimes and therefore can only be unique. When you tap into the original crystalline essence of your soul, you will know this to be true for you. The path less travelled is chosen by few, accepted by even less and completed rarely. However once you commence down the road of remembering your spirit, there is no retreat; there is no exit or turn off signs. You just need to keep on going within your-self and you will find that with practice and application you will find more loving and easier practices as you go.

We all live in a well constructed, ordered world where we are conditioned to our sense of normality depending on where we find ourselves. This programming re-ignites in each incarnation from the moment of conception right through to the point of realisation when we begin questioning the real purpose of our lives. I have not met one person in this life that is not seeking something outside of themselves that has greater meaning in their quest for a better way of life. Within each of us exists the eternal spark of our spirit patiently awaiting our recognition and acceptance. It is this spirit that provides life, sustains us when we are tested and is the key to attaining real meaning in your life. This is the spirit often demonstrated by humanity in times of disaster and chaos when we need each other. It seems this same spirit is rarely on show during the good, prosperous times when every person just looks after themselves. It is interesting that we tend to learn more from our mistakes and drama than we do when things are going well or do we just like to make our lives harder than they have to be?

While I had a passing curiosity in spirituality, I was always fearful of losing control of my-self and my life to energies or beings beyond my ability to reason and logic away. Well I did lose control massively in 1998 when I ended my marriage which triggered the loss of my beautiful children, my friends and associates, my career and just about all of my possessions. Having lost my own parents in my teenage years, deciding to leave my marriage was the most painstaking decision I had ever made as it had an enormous impact on others, most particularly my children. I never really thought that I could make this choice and when I broke the news to my children, I may as well have told them that I was dying and this is a moment that I can never take back. It is hard to imagine the pain and hardship this created for everyone and I pray that with time they can accept and understand my choices.

Unfortunately this story is too familiar in our world and I live everyday with the consequences of my choices. There are always alternate choices and I do not believe that any of us make choices that will intentionally create unnecessary pain and suffering. However our choices are limited by the information and consciousness we have at the time. We make numerous choices in every moment of every day. Some of these choices we make consciously, although most are automatic, sub-consciously programmed choices. It is these choices that influence our state of mind, our mood, our physicality, our relationships, our roles and the quality of our lives. We are led to believe in our upbringing, our education, our qualifications and experiences, in the feedback received from others. Rarely do we believe in or even hear the inner knowing that whispers from our intuitive selves.

Everyone is searching for meaning and purpose for this life to create some measure of control over the life that you are living. Life has order and is predictable however it is not as structured or controllable as we would like to think. We may like to think that we can control nature and control our nature in a physical sense and this may be so. However if you do not give consideration to the nature of your spirit you are dismissing the essence of all life for it is your spirit that inspires and energises all existence. Everything is made up of this energy; everything in all existence consists of the same energy, is inter-connected and is therefore reliant on one another. When we fully comprehend that we all exist within the one body of energy, connected and communicating in every way, you will know who you are and why you are here. Everyone, everybody, everything is here for a purpose and has their role to play in all things whether you are human, animal, nature, the planet, a star, a galaxy or space. You just need to determine where you fit within this existence and play your role to the best of your ability. Every choice every day will positively or negatively affect your life and the lives of others, so choose consciously with considerate wisdom. When you begin to know who you really are, you will hopefully be able to make better informed choices creating no harm for your-self or others in the process.

We all have a story to tell about lives well lived and in sharing our stories and our experiences we may prompt another into remembering who they are. My story is ordinary and is replicated all over our world in various forms. I was born in 1959 a middle child in a large Catholic family in outback Australia and had a carefree, but disciplined traditional childhood until both parents died five years apart during my teenage years. The death of our parents had an enormous impact on my life and family which led to the forming of many of my-self destructive and dysfunctional patterns and behaviours that lasted for the next thirty years. For many years of my life, I had little regard for my-self or anyone else for that matter and I did not care whether I lived or died. I had shut my-self down, lost all belief in most things including religion, partied hard, lived selfishly and saw little purpose in being here. This period of my life is now a little blurry and I was very fortunate to survive without any significant lasting damage through this drunken haze. My angels and guides have worked very hard to keep me here, so there must be a reason.

According to the program many of us live by, I married in my early twenties, built our home, focused on career, education and played a role in creating three beautiful children. The birth of these wonderful spirits re-ignited my spark of life through the overwhelming sense of love that I felt for and from them. I had often described this love as the ultimate willingness to lay my own life down before allowing any harm to come to my children. This is an incredible parental instinct presenting an unselfish glimpse of love however I found that it was not total love. Many of us talk about having unconditional love for our children, but I have always been challenged in being able to give unconditional love that I did not have within my-self. I knew that the love I felt with my children was real although I did not feel this love was present in other aspects of my life and this left me wanting. Many parents feel this love and sometimes live vicariously through their children, which places enormous pressure on their own relationships. In the west we seem to believe that when we have the ideal occupation providing the great income, we can provide for our children and partner and then we will be set for life. Been there, done that, didn't work. I now know that money, relationships and possessions do not define our spirit nature, in fact they often disguise and confuse our meaning of real success. It is only when you fully know and love all of your-self, can you look after your relationship which in turn looks after the children and work just sustains your physicality, it is not your purpose.

To experience real love we need to be open to receive love firstly from ourselves and this is the overflowing love that we can share with others. Most of us have little experience of this love and this limits our ability to accept this love even when it wraps itself around our hearts. All I knew at the time is that I had not experienced this level of love, even from my parents, and this started an adventure that is still ongoing. It begins with the journey of self discovery through getting to know the real you. Consider for a moment—can you really know what you do not feel, can you accept what you do not know, can you trust what you do not accept, can you embrace what you do not trust, can you love what you do not embrace and can you be what you do not love? When most of us do not know how to feel, how can we feel our knowing of ourselves to know who we really are? Without this real sense of ourselves, how is it then possible for us to accept, trust, embrace, love and be who we really are or share this love with anyone else for that matter? This is the great human dilemma and paradox where we are all searching for what already exists inside of us. Love is not something received from outside of ourselves. Love is the prime energy of who you really are, it exists in your pure feelings and rises from deep within the source of our soul. Love is your sense of absolute personal freedom that liberates your soul to experience its true self in this physical form.

Each of us is a unique representation of spirit in this human form, shaped and influenced by every experience in every lifetime we have experienced consciously or sub-consciously. Consider that you have lived for many thousands of lifetimes and that you have evolved through the whole range of human experiences to reach this point of your consciousness. You have acquired many gifts and skills to share with your-self and others, all you have to do is to go within, reconnect with your soul and let the gifted beauty of your true self emerge. You will be pleasantly surprised, I know that I was. Your soul source is real, it is whole, it is connected and it is love.

It is also interesting that you will find that your past will not feel quite real, nor will you be able to identify with your former selves. You may even feel like you have passed from one life to another without losing the memory of your former life. Each time you go through a significant shift in your life, it may seem like another lifetime. This has been my experience and it is not a defence or avoidance mechanism. Your memories also run on programs, selectively storing and retrieving the information that suits the purpose of your mind to hold you wherever it chooses. In connecting with your soul's essence you will begin to see your mind as the wonderful, enabling energy that it is. You will also observe how it can restrict and limit your spiritual growth. The programming of the mind and society is generally not about liberation and soul expression, it is about control, order and servility. When you step into the full power of your soul, be aware that everyone will not see your world as you see it and it is not your role to convince them otherwise. Just walk the truth of your soul with purpose and allow others to be.

KNOWING SPIRIT

These Symbols of the Universe represent keys to your consciousness written in language your soul understands even if your intellect is still challenged by this possibility. You do not need to believe in these symbols for them to work, they are designed to by-pass any intellectual programming, blockages or limitations to find their way to the core energy that needs attention. When you spend time working with these symbols, you will unlock the truth of your spirit that is your true self. It will be like you have just received the keys to the infinite energy of universal knowing inside of your-self. Allow your-self time to explore and experiment with the symbols to determine how they may work best for you. Trust that you will know what you are doing for this is not the first time you have been here. Be with these symbols to know your-self and re-discover the beautiful being of pure love, light and truth that you really are. You have embraced your spiritual journey of remembering who you are to release the full potential of your soul's evolution. You just need to let go of needing to know every step of the way and surrender to the energy of your soul.

Through my journey within my-self, I have communed with many spiritual guides, teachers, divine spirit, angels, ascended masters, star and light beings of greater universal consciousness. During this discourse, I have received many insights into the human condition and the challenge of fully integrating our light bodies within this dense physical form. While in a meditative space, I have experienced supreme consciousness where I have been guided to my purpose and the purpose of humanity. We are all here to clear our fears and negativity to love and live the consciousness that is our spirit regardless of what tribe, country or belief system we were born into. We truly live within the garden of paradise that is earth and when we realise that we are as much of the earth as we are of spirit, fully integrated living lovingly connected to all existence we will know who we truly are. Life is meant to be easy, loving, simple, positive, honourable and with abundance for all to share. Each soul has the freedom and responsibility to create this reality; it is just a matter of being who you truly are.

Over the last half century, I have studied, experienced and learnt varying philosophies, theories, beliefs and practices from many powerful souls to develop my own creed for living my life. As with all truths and beliefs that are in a constant state of evolution, you will adapt, reinvent and create new processes to serve and honour your journey along your way. These are the principles of my spiritual truth that I strive to live by in every moment:

My Spiritual Truth

I am Spirit

I am a spirit having this human experience. I am not a human being having a spiritual experience. My spirit is infinitely travelling through all space and time. My soul energy is eternally connected to all the knowing energy of the universe.

Be the Best of Spirit

I am here to be the best loving and positive spirit I can be in physical form in this lifetime and this is the energy I share with everyone and everything. I share my love through living this love in all I am and in all I do.

One Lifetime, Many Experiences, Many Lifetimes, One Experience

My spirit incarnated on earth in this human form. Each incarnation contributes to the next incarnation, so every life experience is an investment. If you desire to create a particular energy, gift or skill, start now for you will achieve what you set your intention toward. Be aware of your seed or core motivation to sow your intentions with love and honour. When you deal with your life as it presents itself to you in this lifetime, you will have dealt with this energy in every life through all time.

Consciousness = Vibration

The only thing I take into my next life is my conscious energy which determines the quality and experiences of each life. Our consciousness connects with the parents we choose to the patterns and behaviours we are here to heal and clear. You are meant to be free of all fear and negativity to be the truth of your love and positivity.

My Life is My Creation

Each life experience reflects my attitude and ability to create what I really desire in my life. Every decision we make is an act of creativity from the time we awaken to the moment we sleep. As I can dream and imagine, I can create consciously and freely.

Light Motivation

All energy is pure light from which love and fear emerge as our primary motivators for all we do. All our intentions, actions and experiences can be traced to these source energies. Know your source and you will know your light.

Love Overcomes Fear

Each soul experiences who they are not through fear and negativity to be the loving, positive energy of who they are. There seems little avoiding this, just walk through the falsehood and shallowness of your fears to feel the loving, joyful courage and pure intent of your heart. There is always a loving answer when you feel your way. Remember—Powerful souls create powerfully—either negatively or positively.

Befriend Pain

All discord, fear, negativity, disease, pain, conflict, tension, stress and regret in your life are indicators that you have taken the more challenging path to understand more about who you really are not in order to find your true self. When you accept, make peace and really love your pain, you will heal the energy that created this imbalance. Fighting fear with fear feeds this fear. Positive love is your healing solution.

I am Responsible

I am totally responsible for everything I feel, think, say and do in my life to create loving goodness and I enable all others to be responsible for themselves. I am not responsible for others nor do others do anything to me that I have not created at some level in any lifetime. Self-responsibility empowers and sets your energy free.

Real Feelings

Our experiences are based on our core feelings about ourselves and the realness of the energy of who we really are. As you feel about your self is how you relate and create with others. Your feelings are pure insights of truth just before you engage your mind-based emotions. Your feelings will always be loving, positive, honouring, simple and easy for you to understand and follow. Your mind generally will not.

Love is Freedom

To experience real love, you need to really feel your soul senses, know intimately, trust totally, accept freely and embrace wholly all of your-self to know your love. How you love your self is how you will be able to love others and as you love you, you will love others through your love of who you truly are. This is real and eternal.

Love in the Living

How you love your-self, your body, others and the planet is all connected. Be aware of how you treat all of your-self for you need to support you through every lifetime. We do not let go of discord when we kill off each body. Loving you = healthy mind + healthy body + happy spirit = a great life and so your energy grows. It is all one.

Spiritual Innocence

Remember to have real fun, lighten up, love openly and freely, have honourable intentions and always be true to who you really are and be the best spirit you can be. It is okay to be your-self. Your spirit is childlike, loving, in the moment, free, pure, open, imaginative, creative, connected, innocent, interested, involved and beautiful. Just as you would never harm or poison a child, you should not harm your spirit.

Purpose for Being

Our collective soul purpose is to live the truth of our spirit in this physical form. Can you imagine a world where we all live lovingly, honourably, caring, sharing and connected to the infinite bounty of this beautiful living evolving planet? This is the paradise we have sought forever to create and all of spirit is here to support this universal quest. This is the spiritual responsibility of living your beautiful life.

SPIRITUAL HEALING

The innate ability to heal energetically and physically exists within each of us. When you know that you are a spirit having this human experience, you will know that your body is the vehicle that enables you to experience the truth of your spirit through this physical form. Your body is the sensory mechanism through which you feel life, taste, smell, experience and receive all the physical spiritual gifts this magnificent planet of the universe has to offer. You create life through your body and life creates you from within. As you experience this and every life, you are creating your reality through your soul body consciously feeling and evolving through every experience. You take on all of your experiences in every cell in your body just as the universe takes on all the energy of every soul experience in all of existence. There is no separation or isolation in all existence. There is just energy vibrating and evolving to the best of its ability and we all have our unique roles to play in this process regardless of how small or insignificant we feel that may be. There is no escape from this reality.

It all starts within ourselves and our recognition that our soul is the core energy of our physical body. When you acknowledge your soul's energy and its infinite ability, you will begin to know who you really are. For too long we have accepted what we have been taught about physicality, spirituality, life, tradition and social normality only to reach a point where this reality loses its appeal, meaning and purpose. When comfortable normality no longer appears to be so, you will begin to question the reality of everything. If only we could put aside our dogmatic or even pragmatic beliefs and accept that just maybe there is more to life than we can see, prove and document, we might discover greater meaning and improve the quality of life along the way. Science and spirituality are intrinsically linked, they are one and the same, if only we realised that we are all part of the same body, serving the same purpose.

There are many healing and belief processes available for you to find your way and I will share with you one method that I found useful in getting to know my-self. Commence by going deep within your-self to get to know and understand who you are. You are not your role, status, qualification or your physicality. You are far greater than all of your achievements put together. Find a quite, positive space to create a loving atmosphere of serenity and healing. Lay down either on the floor, massage table or bed in comfortable clothing and place your hands on your-self asking your universal energy to come through you into your hands. If you do not have a process for this, imagine or visualise your-self as a being of pure light totally connected to all energy around you, flowing through you in a continuous loop.

You will start to feel your energy running through your hands to feel you, to feel how your energy feels and begin to feel the physical nature of your spirit which can be a wonderful, enlightening experience. Allow your-self time and space to get to know this energetic experience of your-self and spend real time building your relationship with your-self, possibly for the first time in many lifetimes. You are not what others think of you nor are you defined by your relationships. You are uniquely you, shaped by every lifetime experience you have been through. Invest your energy in getting to know all of your-self (both the light and shade) just as you would when you are building relationships with others. You will be pleasantly and confidently surprised in knowing the beautiful, loving being that you have always known your-self to be.

This experience can show you how relatively simple and easy it is to access the true nature of your spirit. We all have the capacity to create real magic in our lives if only we would allow our controlling mind the space and permission to surrender to the will of our divinity. Through knowing all aspects of your-self, you will have a greater understanding of your primary motivators and enablers of your energetic flow or restrictions. Once you know your-self, you will be able to take back your power from everyone and everything, including your own traditional and spiritual belief systems.

Who you are is a pure, loving being of infinite energy and truth connected to all knowing existence through time and space. You are as the creator intended, as the Supreme Being is, in the body of all there is and you contain all the love, wisdom, power and energy of the entire universe within you. Connect with who you really are, connect with the energy of this planet and you will connect with all the energy of the universe. I have detailed below the process I utilised to get to know who I am and now share with anyone who is seeking their truth. At your own pace try this process, experiment within you and you will be amazed at the real power of you.

Tree Visualisation—Place your hands on your **Root Chakra** situated at your groin and imagine your-self as a tree, let this tree present itself to you, observe what the tree looks like, the trunk, branches, leaves and its root system—is it balanced and healthy, strong and vibrant. Feel how you feel as a tree, how connected are you, is your root system strong and how is your energy flowing? Feel how connected you feel, how still you are and how conscious you are of your surroundings. Take your roots deep into the earth's core, feel the molten powerful energy of the planet (feel how similar it is to the Sun's energy) enter your roots and draw this energy through the earth, through all of your energy centres, your chakras and out through your crown. Take this energy as far out into the universe as you can imagine and loop it back through the other side of the earth and back through the centre forming a continuous loop of infinite energy flow through all existence. Feel how this energy connects you to your-self, the planet and all there is and observe any changes within the tree and your-self. This is your connection to all consciousness and when you are connected wherever you are; your energy runs right through the planet and through all space and time. Walking with this consciousness will assist your-self and all others who share your journey with you including this planet and the universe. Connect with your body on earth and you will be connected to the universe. If you perform no other spiritual role other than being this connection, you will have shared your universal energy with the entire planet wherever you are.

Loving Relationship with Self—How often do you hear about the concept of self love although we are rarely taught about how or what you need to do to truly love you and have a loving relationship with your-self. Love is often defined as a feeling or something you receive from outside of your-self or from another. This is partially true however if you do not feel or act loving toward or within your-self, receiving this energy from another will be extremely challenging. We are all love, that is a universal truth and all you need to do is to remember and accept this truth. Are you really loving you with everything you ingest, where you live and work, in your relationships and through the joy and compassion you share with your-self and others? These very honest questions are necessary for you to commence really loving your-self for honesty is the basis of all prosperous relationships, starting with how honest you really are with your-self.

Place your hands on your **Sacral Chakra** on your navel and visualise your-self as either the male or female you (whatever sex comes to mind first), observe what you look like, what you are doing and how you feel. Feel this being for it is the male/female aspect of you. Then visualise your-self as the complementary being, female or male, observe what you look like, what you are doing and how you feel for this is this aspect of you. These beings can be your-self, someone you know or from another time or space. What they look like is not important, how they feel is. Once you have felt the individual energies, have them look upon one another and feel how they feel about each other as this will give you some indication about how you feel about these aspects of your-self. Have them come together in a loving embrace and observe how they feel and whether their collective energy changes at all for this is your adult relationship. This relationship with your-self will reflect all other relationships in your life and this can change every day. It is from this chakra that you create and carry the impact of all relationships.

When you have experienced the male (intellectual) and female (intuitive) aspects of you, call in the child you, this will be either sex at any age, observe what the child looks like, what it is doing and how it feels. After you have felt this individual energy, observe what the child thinks and feels about the adult you, both male and female. Feel the child's energy then allow the adults to feel what they feel about the child you. Allow the child to embrace both the adults and feel how this feels for this is your complete relationship with your-self, all aspects of you, the male, female and child are your holy trinity in this existence. They are all of you, the thinking, courageous, practical, action oriented masculine you and the feeling, caring, nurturing, intuitive, loving feminine you. When the adult you can really relate to one another, they will enable life to be safe for the imaginative, creative, playful, free, loving, in the moment, spirit child you to emerge. You have never grown out of your child self, you have always been with you, waiting patiently for you to find the time to be who you really are. Ironically you have known this all along. In order to fit in with your illusionary world, you have just grown around your-self, moulded your-self to fit with others, sacrificing and compromising your-self and your aspirations to please and serve others. Now is the time for you to be all of your-self and to allow your-self to play lovingly, creatively and freely in this life. Your inner child needs the adult male and female you to be wise, loving and together to feel safe to be free. This is who you are and the adult you needs to create a safe, nurturing environment to support your way.

Be Responsible for You. The gateway bridging the physical and spiritual exists within our **Solar Plexus Chakra**, place your hands just below the rib cage and simply repeat this affirmation three times:-

"I am totally responsible for my-self and I enable all others to be totally responsible for themselves".

This declaration will set you free from external distractions and obligations that have effectively restricted your energy flow for many lifetimes. When you are able to concentrate on your feelings, your reactions, your responses to life you will be able to really know you, what turns you on and off in life and be able to use your feelings to guide you on your true path. When you are caught up in other's dramas, trying to rescue, save or fix another without really knowing you, you will shut down your own energy field, taking on their burdens while crippling their ability to know and be responsible for themselves. You are not selfish by focusing on what you are about and it is only through knowing all of your-self will you truly be able to show others their way. Every soul has ultimate responsibility for their soul's energy and only when they know themselves can they know another. Otherwise we remain locked into each other's energy fields, confusing and limiting everyone.

There are many myths and traditional beliefs held about spirituality that may have worked for who you were not in the past. I know from my experiences within my-self and with many others that we are all unique and special beings of light. We have all journeyed through time and space in our own way acquiring many gifts and profound knowing about life and our purpose. You can only know you from your own experience of spirit life. Others can attempt to explain you from their own perspective and experiences, however only you can really know all of you.

When you have completed this process with your physical chakras, your spiritual chakras situated at the heart, throat, third-eye and crown will open to receive you. Place your hands on each Chakra in the following order:-

Heart Chakra—feel the enormity of your own love energy, filling your heart with your love to share this overflowing and infinite energy with others.

Throat Chakra—feel your expressive creative centre open, connected to your heart's love, creating and expressing yourself openly and freely.

Third Eye Chakra—feel your all seeing, all knowing intuitive eye open, enabling access to all your spiritual senses to see, feel and hear all.

Crown Chakra—open the flow of your energy to the flow of the universal energy that you are, connected, whole and complete. Trust your knowing.

Allow sufficient time and experience for you to assimilate and integrate this energy within your being and you will really be able to feel yourself and others. Repeat this process as often as you wish, get to know all of you and you will have your answers.

When you know your-self, you will know your way.

BACKGROUND OF THE SYMBOLS

During my spiritual journey within my-self, I studied and explored many different belief systems, spiritual and physical, massage and energy healing processes. I spent considerable time with a wide variety of spiritual teachers, psychics, mediums and read everything I could on metaphysics to gain a greater understanding about my spiritual life. The one belief I have retained right throughout my life is that we continually evolve through many lifetimes by the process of reincarnation. This knowing has been with me since I can remember providing insights into the diversity and uniqueness of every individual presiding on this earth plane. Apart from vagaries of my lost teenage years following the death of my parents, I have always accepted that there is an omnipresent being or body that exists greater than the sum of ourselves. There is a purpose behind all creation, everything is connected, inter-reliant and involved in the greater evolution of all existence.

Instead of dismissing or neglecting my long held beliefs, my journey has solidified and broadened my acceptance of the omniscient energy of the universe. You will find that every experience, your programmed learning and knowing combine to provide a multi-dimensional and flexible ever-evolving view of spiritual life in this human form. For you are a spirit having a human experience, not a human having a spiritual experience and when you accept this truth, you will begin to understand why you are here. During my corporate life I had many unexplained experiences and was also exposed to many different personal, management and life philosophies. These experiences challenged my view of life and began the questioning process that continues until this day. There were many times where I discussed and knew information beyond my field of experience or knowledge. The more frequently these events occurred, the greater I trusted these instincts instead of just accepting my programmed knowledge. It is interesting to now reflect that my General Manager once told me that I was highly intuitive and should trust this instinctive knowing and not second guess my-self. I am not sure he even knew the extent of this comment and how it would shape my journey. Ironically he was the same person who ended my career. I blessed him then and was very grateful for his initial recognition of my talents and for his dysfunctional actions finally dissolving the illusion of my corporate life.

In letting go of all I held dear at the time, I was seriously challenged and felt enormous stress of not knowing what was coming next. As a result, I created a serious illness for my-self and even thought for a time that I was losing my mental capacity. This was the beginning of my healing journey. For the first time in my life I treated my-self to a massage, not just any massage, a very special energetic massage which opened the access to my sensory body. I met some very unique healers and my Reiki healer and teacher. My only intention at the time was to know my-self better and to resolve many old issues and patterns inside of myself. Before leaving the corporate world, I attended a comprehensive healing process called "The Hoffman Process" that examined every aspect of the self, the physical, spiritual, intellectual and emotional, stripping all bare to reach the core of your-self. If I thought I had been tested previously, this was the real test for I discovered elements of my-self and my life that I had previously not been aware of and I was mortified. So much so that I was willing my-self out of this life as I had seen my core issue for this life. Without going into morbid details, this process laid out everything for honest and critical examination and release. The facilitators graciously and compassionately guided you through the process of letting go of the unnecessary patterns and habits to commence the process of reconstructing the beautiful beings that we are meant to be. Against their best advice, I only lasted about 2 hours back at work before I quit forever. I just could not live another moment being who I was not. I left the corporate world, left the city with my partner at the time and moved to the Sunshine Coast to rediscover who I wanted to be when I grew up.

About three months later on New Year's Eve 2000, I completed a sculpture course at the Woodford Folk Festival and absolutely loved it. When I returned to the coast, I went looking for a sculpture teacher and I was advised to teach my-self as there were no teachers here at that time. After obtaining some man-made hebel stone, I created some sculptures for my-self and just seemed to instinctively know what to do.

I had combined my limited knowledge of sculpture and Reiki healing to create a thank you gift for my Reiki teacher and other key people in my life. Little did I know that this would start a very special business and way of life that continues to this day, 11 years later. I created eastern style sculptures, Universal PowerPoles with Reiki, Siechem and Sanskrit Symbols inscribed upon them to energise and clear the environments in which they were placed. I thought we had it made when I did my first market under a palm tree on a beautiful Sunshine Coast beach, where we sold a few pieces and received my first commission. It was there that my craft was borne and fostered into what you are reading today. I have since created over 10000 sculptures and other products that have found their way right throughout the world, creating and amplifying positive loving energy wherever they are placed.

Within six months of regularly attending markets and spiritual festivals in Australia, I started to clearly see shapes and symbols when I was sculpting in my shed. These symbols were promptly scribbled in pencil on the wall along with the meanings I had received for each symbol. I did nothing with these symbols until I was reading a book I had ordered months earlier and there was one of the symbols I had on the wall along with the same meaning that I had received. This may have been a co-incidence or chance, although I took it as a sign of something greater. I still did nothing with these new symbols until one of the last festivals I was doing that year in 2001, when I finally had the courage and conviction to begin to place these symbols on a few sculptures to see how they would be received by people. Well did I find out quickly. These were the first sculptures to sell out and people could not purchase them fast enough and in fact we sold out at that festival. As with any time you work with powerful energies particularly in group situations like festivals, your energy is amplified and you are accelerated on your journey. Well this did occur after the festival was over and that night even though I was completely exhausted in every way, I could not sleep and channelled another 25 new symbols.

Little did I know that this weekend would be the beginning of the end of my relationship at the time. These symbols had come for my healing and would initiate and accelerate my spiritual journey even though I struggled to accept this reality. When my partner decided that she needed to honour her journey and explore another path in her life, this really triggered off a series of events that have shaped my gift to this day. Even though I had prophesied this possibility, I can quite honestly admit that I was again seriously challenged to the point of not wanting to be here. Until you really experience the darkest remnants of your soul, you have no idea of how strong and capable you are. It was through this experience that I realised why I had been given these symbols and began to accept that my gift was here for me to rediscover and remember the truth of who I truly am and this process is ongoing. Once more I had created the experience that I needed to heal.

With this realisation I started to consciously use the symbols that I had previously received to really understand what they did and know how they worked. To my amazement, I was pleasantly surprised during meditation, doing healing work on my-self, in my sleep and while working on new sculptures I started to feel these energies release and energise within me. As I progressed on this journey, I became more conscious of what I was doing to create the reality I was experiencing. While working with the symbols, I was able to call for additional symbols to work on new blockages, restrictions or opportunities and they started to come in thick and fast. There were many times when I received far more symbols than I could remember and record. The symbols in this publication are the symbols I have received and worked with over the last 11 years. They are also only a fraction of the infinite symbols of the universe available for our loving use.

As I actively worked with the symbols I felt unique feelings that I had not felt before, started to know things previously unknown to me and gained insights into my life and many of the challenges of humanity. It was like all of a sudden I really began to connect with my essence, with spirit, with the universe and as a result gained access to a wealth of energetic knowing that I did not previously have access to. From being in a position of self created despair and hopelessness, I arose feeling about my true self in a way that I had not felt before. I was beginning to get to know who I really was, who I had always been and I really liked and loved who I had found. It was like I had come home to my true self, the being I always felt that I was although did not always know how to acknowledge or be. This was the start of a beautiful, loving and lasting relationship with my soul self and this will always be worthwhile.

Through this process of creativity, following my intuitive knowing, I had found my way back to the truth of my heart. I now cherish every person and every experience that has led me back to my-self and I encourage everyone to honour their journey and their intuition. As you release your truth you enable all others to release their truth, activating true and honest energy all around you. This is the energy we are meant to follow and nurture for any false energy no matter how often it is repeated can never become the truth. All energy must have substance to sustain itself creatively. I know what I have experienced is very real for me and having shared this energy with the other souls I have met, I know the energy and the intent we all share is positive, is loving and is real.

I now know these symbols came to me to bypass my intellectual ability to block and reason away anything that did not make sense, logically and rationally. Humanity has been using symbols since the dawn of time to communicate, to describe, to illustrate the passing of the ages. Like the sense of smell, symbols are unique and open for interpretation by everyone who encounters them. The ancients understood this and as our civilisations have become more organised, controlled and fearful, symbols have unfortunately been relegated to the realms of the occult or today, something to decorate a t-shirt or tattoo. All symbols, logos or signs have real meaning beyond our intellectual ability to grasp or fully understand and not everything needs to be known.

Symbols are very powerful as they resonate with the energy of the universal patterns of all existence. They are keys to a greater realm of consciousness, opening and reminding our souls of their intent and purpose. Your soul knows, your head only thinks it knows. Even if you cannot intellectually conceive of this idea, your soul will know as it remembers all that is true. Your human programming and limitations will do their best to resist you opening to all of your-self however persist and you too will be amazed by your results. If you consider that you only utilise 10% of your intelligence consciously, your super-consciousness' access to universal knowing is the other 90% that we rarely acknowledge. I was no different before I consciously started down this path, if I could not rationalise, understand or prove it logically, than it was not worth knowing. The "prove it to believe it" philosophy that has dominated our creativity since the middle ages has seriously limited our access to our greater power of the universe that exists in all things. All theories and philosophies through time have been continually tested and challenged as we evolve and strive to understand more of this life.

We are what we think, we see what we know and we believe what we wish to believe and this is all true, but is it working? Are we living in harmony, sustainably and with loving consideration for all things in peaceful balance? For a species to believe that it dominates all life and that all resources are solely here to satisfy our insatiable needs is surely deluded, if not misguided. Our physical lives are limited to the life of each body, our souls passing through each lifetime accumulating its gifts and wounds, experiencing and expressing its spirit through this physical form. This process is repeated through all forms of life here on this planet and through all time and space. With this realisation you will understand the inter-connectedness of all things and that everything has its role to play. Intellectually we struggle to conceive all existence, the size, shape and purpose of the ever evolving and expanding universe. All we know is that we are here right now doing what we do the best we can, trying to make sense of everything. The only answer you need is—what makes sense to you and this will be your truth.

WORKING WITH THE SYMBOLS

Each of these Universal Symbols contained here act as keys to your consciousness, unlocking, releasing or amplifying the essential energy of your spirit. Each symbol plays its role activating its energy on many levels enabling you to access elements of your-self that you may have long forgotten, neglected, abused or dismissed. These keys will assist you to find your opportunities or solutions. With applied practice, you will find this process easier than you could imagine and the answers to the issues that challenge us are usually found in our contrary behaviours or beliefs. These symbols are very powerful, simple and easy to use. All you have to do is to let go of any preconceived ideas or reservations you may have about their effectiveness and give your-self permission to have an experience of your soul. There are no guarantees that this form of energy will work for you or that you will have immediate life changing or profound experiences. You will be positively altered in some way, even on a subtle level deep within you and you will start to notice small differences in your approach to life. We are influenced by all the energy that is around us every day and as you become more conscious, you will actively invoke positive, loving change in your life. Your power exists in your ability to believe.

Through my experience, I have found that spirit always communicates to us in very simple, easy, honouring, loving and positive terms. This is how I determine whether my messages are coming from a clear spiritual space or from the complicated, controlling, difficult, obligatory, fearful and negative intellectual human form. We have all been programmed over many lifetimes to believe that just because life has always been full of conflict, drama, fear, lack, politics, suffering, hardship and negativity, that this is the way it will always be. You need to get others before they get you, look after yourself, acquire all the possessions you can, climb to the top of the heap, compete, strive, win, get a good job, it is all about the family, tribe, cult, religion, company and so on the constant struggle goes, you get the drift here for you have experienced it all before. My observation of life has been borne of many similar experiences, not all pretty or flattering to the soul. As I have continued on my spiritual journey over the last decade, I have not seen a profound shift in our evolution as a species, although I live lovingly and eternally in hope.

I have been involved with many people who have resumed responsibility for themselves, commenced their journey of self-discovery and seen the enormous improvements in the quality of their lives as a result of their inner work. Every one of us will find our way eventually. When we realise that our answers do not exist in someone or something else, we will find that our spirit's answers exist inside each one of us. With the actualisation of this realisation, the truth of each soul contributes to the greater consciousness of the entire universe. Each of us is a unique spark of spirit, each cultivated and nurtured by the experience of many lifetimes, all especially gifted with a significant role to play. What is your role, your gift, your contribution? Have you found your-self and your answers yet? Now is your time if you are ready. Read on and you may find out just a little more about who you really are.

You can read this material from cover to cover or just open randomly on the page that draws you on a particular day. This information seeks to inspire and ignite the flame of spirit that you are and only you can know how it can help you. I encourage you to experiment and play with these symbols and concepts to feel what works effectively for you. The symbols are programmed to transmute all negativity and fear into loving, positive energy so no harm can come to you nor can you cause any harm with them. As we are all uniquely similar, each of us is drawn to and utilise energy for what we need in our own way. It is okay for you to be different, special and unique for this is who you are. We are all different and we are meant to be this diverse representation of spirit in this human form. Celebrate your uniqueness for you should not hide the true nature of your-self any longer.

How I came to intrinsically know the symbols and received their meanings was through spending countless hours working and playing with them on many levels. The process I use for working with the symbols is:

- Find a quiet peaceful, comfortable space to meditate on a symbol

- Select the symbol you wish to work with (randomly or by choice)
- Resist the urge to read or intellectualise the symbol by reading the words
- Focus on the symbol until it goes blurry before your eyes
- Shut your eyes and the imprint of the symbol will be visible behind your eyelids
- Allow the symbol to go where it wishes to go within your body
- As the symbol finds its way, you may feel tingles, warmth or odd sensations
- Let the symbol rest where it wishes and observe what you are feeling
- As you sit with the symbol, you may feel energy release inside your body
- Through this release you may receive some clarity about the energy, any blockages, restrictions, beliefs, wounds, habits, gifts or opportunities that are within you
- With this clarity within your consciousness, you now have the ability to take appropriate action to clear, resolve, let go, heal, amplify or accelerate your energy
- When you feel it is time, open your eyes and reflect on what you have experienced
- You are now conscious of a particular aspect of that issue which may need to be dealt with or faced again now you have greater awareness of your-self
- Remember always that you have all the knowledge of the universe within you, all you have to do is find your access to this connection with you—you truly are your source.
- Action is the key to all change, when you listen to your intuitive knowing, acknowledge and act upon your guidance, you will be open to greater clarity
- If you do not receive any insights immediately, be patient for you have released your intention to find clarity within your-self—allow time for you to adjust
- Frustration, confusion and exacerbation always precede enlightenment.

By working with these symbols or any other energy you will change your life, your beliefs and your behaviours. Do not be alarmed or concerned if your reality does not appear to be real to you any more as you have just shifted your perspective. Your life has not changed, you have. It is important to remain grounded within the earth by keeping your-self connected to the natural world. Spend conscious time in your garden, by being creative, sitting in a park or walking in a forest, do anything that really connects you to the planet. As you connect with your body drawing your energy through the earth you will be totally connected to the universe. The earth is always connected and conscious of its relationship with all existence.

Also be patient with change, do not try to change all your life in an instance. Take your time and remember that the spiritual journey is much like pushing water down hill so go with your flow. You have spent lifetimes reaching this point in your consciousness, allow sufficient time to integrate your new knowing and assimilate the new you within your environment. You are just beginning to know who you are so allow time for others to get to know who you are without imposing your views or new beliefs on anyone. Just because you have found something that works for you, everyone is in their own space in their own time and need to be nurtured to their own truth. Just be your true self, be loving in all that you are and share freely with those who invite you to. It would be great if everyone got this immediately, but it will take time. Just be the change you wish to see in the world. Create your reality into what you wish it to be, share with the people who wish to share your energy and from there you will share with the entire planet. Be the ripple of positive, loving change you wish to experience all around you and this is the energy that will come back to you in great abundance. The only being you can change or influence is your-self.

Each of the symbols contained here act as keys to your consciousness, unlocking, releasing or amplifying the essential energy of your spirit. Each symbol plays its role activating its energy on many levels enabling you to access elements of your-self that you may have forgotten, neglected, abused or dismissed to find your opportunity or solution. With applied practice, you will find this process easier than you could imagine and the answers to the issues that challenge us are usually found in alternative behaviours or beliefs. To change you need to be different, think differently and act differently. The universal world will not change to suit you. You are the focal point of your life and the soul recipient of your evolution. Always remember that your positive loving answers will always overcome any negative, fearful problem. Fighting fear or pain with fear just feeds the fear accelerating the dramatic painful learning impact of our experience. It is not just some trite clichéd response or delusion. Love truly is your answer to most of the dramas of modern life. Try love, it works. We have done fear and negativity to death.

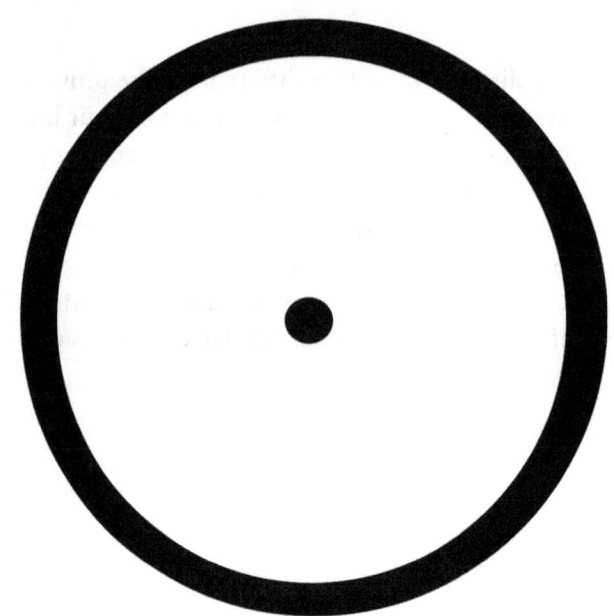

I AM SPIRIT

Who you are is pure spirit. You have come from infinity and you are travelling through infinity. When you accept that you are of the universe and have all the elements of the universe within you, you will know why you have chosen to experience your consciousness in this physical form. You have never really lost sight of who you are. There has always been an eternal light within you guiding you on your path. You have known this truth all along even in your darkest moments of despair and anguish. It has been this light that has sustained you and carried you through every moment you have endured and evolved through. Regardless of each situation you have created, you are always capable of finding your way back to you.

Listen to your inner voice of wisdom, your inner knowing and you will know who you really are and why you are here. You do know you. All you have to do is listen to your soul. You are your universe, your source energy, your infinite knowing, your entire existence. Your experience of life, your frame of reference, your perspective is uniquely your own. You have been shaped by every lifetime you have lived and sculptured by every experience you have grown through. You are uniquely you and all of life is in its perfection. Accept that you are okay just the way you are, come back to your truth and be all of the love that you know that you are. You are a beautiful, loving and powerful being of pure love, light and truth. It is time for you to be all of who you truly are.

Love—I am pure spirit expressed through my humanity in every way.

Note: The symbol of Spirit was one of the first symbols I received in 2001 when carving some of my Universal PowerPole sculptures in my shed on Mt Coolum. I had five symbols come to me while channelling Reiki energy into these sculptures and not knowing what to do with them at the time, I drew them on the wall of the shed with their meanings that I had received. About three months later I received a book I had ordered from France that not only contained this symbol but also had the same meaning that I had received. This was a confirmation that I had tuned into another level of my consciousness although it was several months before I really started to use these symbols on my sculptures and more importantly, in my life.

BE IN EACH MOMENT

Be present in the space between each moment for this is the only reality you truly experience. Right here, right now is the only moment that is real for you and each moment, each nanosecond passes extremely quickly. The moment that has just passed is now being processed by your memory, assessed, analysed and compared against previous experiences you may think are still true. With each moment that passes so too does our lives. When you live your life in each moment you will experience and appreciate each golden moment of life that you have created. We are only capable of really processing life as it happens, as there are numerous distractions, messages, stimuli and information constantly seeking our attention. It requires real discipline and focus to be right here, right now, however if you are not present, you will miss your vital signs or messages and your life will fleetingly pass.

As you are aware of every moment of your life you will begin to receive all the gifts, all the bounty this magnificent planet has to share with you. In every infinite moment of our existence we receive guidance, messages, skills and gifts that cultivate and nurture our lives. There are thousands of these individual bits of guidance every day and most of us feel blessed if we receive one or two of these gifts. You need to be present to clearly hear, see and sense your life and how you need to live to honour and stimulate your soul's evolution. When you are present with your spirit immersed fully within your body, you will know your experience of this life, clearing your path to easily and simply find your own way.

The past and the future only exist in your memory and in your imagination. Any legacies, wounds or fears drawn from the past only serve to taint and distort your experience of the present and therefore negatively influence your future experiences. Whenever you place your mind in past events or issues, this is the energy you bring into the now thus shaping and distracting your experience of your current guidance. As much as you can, bring your attention back to now, clear your thoughts of anything that is not right in front of you, listen and observe any signs in your current reality that are seeking your attention. You only ever have each moment to experience and live your life, treasure each moment, every gift and live your life fully with your heart overflowing with love for you.

Love—I am present in every moment, fully here to be the universe.

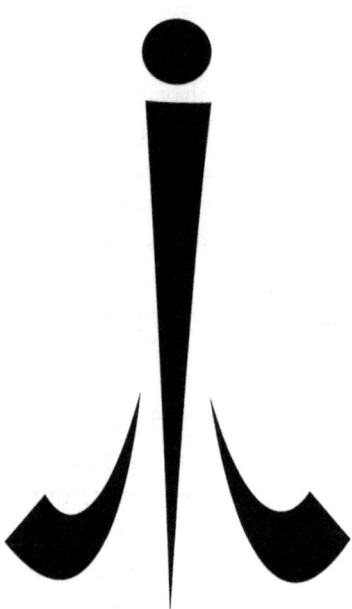

FOCUS ON YOUR SELF

The only being's energy that you fully experience throughout your entire life is your own. No-one else ever fully experiences or knows who you truly are, they only see who you wish to show them which is controlled by how well you know your-self. When you came into this life, you came in alone and you will leave this life by your-self, taking no-one or no-thing with you. It is a good idea that at some time in your life to invest some effort focusing on your-self. The vibration that determines each lifetime is shaped by how conscious, how clear and aware we are and how lovingly we live our lives in every way. We are not our roles, relationships, possessions or status and we are certainly not what others may think of us, for our judgements are just reflections of what we think of ourselves.

To really know your-self you need to be able to spend time experiencing your life from within you. Listen to your clear loving feelings in every moment, make your own sense of your experiences, to know what is best for you and how you would like to share with others. You will change your perspective with experience and you will constantly change how you live through that aspect of your-self that you wish to experience next. It is okay for you to walk your life in your own way. When others are demanding or requiring you to look after their needs before you look after your-self, be sure to know how your involvement honours you. Through many lifetimes we have been heavily programmed to be selfless and to be of service. Many of these master servant relationships are still playing out to this day. If you are still serving others to satisfy your own needs, insecurities or dysfunctions without understanding the true nature of your-self, you will be continually challenged and drained by this service. There will be times when you are right to place others needs before your own although you need to be aware to give through your-self and not of your-self. Selfless service will eventually deplete and erode your sense of self. Every experience of your life regardless of how it presents, is here for you to learn to be more of your true self.

With full awareness of your-self, your desires and aspirations, you will clearly know who you are, where you fit and what you are required to do. Live your life through your-self and you will find fulfilment of purpose beyond your wildest dreams.

Love—I am aware of all my life and I share through my-self in every way.

AWAKEN YOUR CONSCIOUSNESS

There is a greater reality waiting for you to open your eyes and your heart to the infinite possibilities of your spirit. When you accept your spiritual essence is at the very core of your being and that you are here to physically experience all of your spirit, you will awaken magnificently to the dawning of your true self. You have all of your life before you to experience, enjoy and share with the beautiful energy, environment and beings of this planet. No matter where you find your-self, you have the ability to change your circumstances, to change your perspective and to improve the quality of your life. Only you can decide how you wish to live your life, how responsible you wish to be and to access the infinite creative energy that you are. The time for denial, ignorance, excuses and procrastination has passed. It is time for your heart to open.

Affluence, position, culture or belief do not control or influence the quality of our lives. You have full control over your-self and your soul's journey. You are totally shaped by your knowing of who you truly are and your awareness of the infinite options that are always present for you to grow. Your life has always been your choice to make. Accept that you are an infinite being of pure spiritual creation and you will become more aware of the numerous choices available to you. Deny the essence of who you are and you will continue to deny the infinite possibilities of your spirit. If you are currently happy and content with your life, your spiritual nature will only serve to amplify this sense of blissful fulfilment.

When you emerge from the fog of who you are not, you will feel like you have awoken from a dream to begin living your dream. Life really is an illusion; our reality is the meaning we give to this existence. Review any aspect of your life, awake or asleep and it will not feel real. Repeating the experience or the story often enough does not make it real, it just repeats the same behaviours, traditions, rituals and results. If this is working for you, stay on your path. If your life is not as you desire it to be, open your eyes, stand up and take action to change how you are living. If you do not wish to continue repeating the same old patterns or processes, you are free, able and empowered to change them. All change starts within each of us and requires us to take total responsibility for all of our lives and to take positive action to make a real difference in our lives. Allow your-self to be free to experience all of your spirit in this life and this is the freedom that you will create.

Love—I am fully aware and accept I am spirit evolving through the infinite possibilities I create in this life.

SHIFTING CONSCIOUSNESS

Every experience in your life is created through the vibration of your consciousness. You can only create from the essence of your-self whether you are aware of who you are or not. Take a moment to honestly reflect on your life experiences from your own perspective and you will be aware of your own contribution through all of your life. All of these experiences have provided you with your inner knowing, broader awareness and programmed learning that constitutes your consciousness. As you become more aware of your-self through your life, you are evolving into who you are meant to be and realise it has all been your creation. Others may have influenced you, however you have created all of who you are today.

We have all travelled through many lifetimes experiencing just about all there is to experience. The fact that you have found your-self where you are in this lifetime supports all you have done thus far to reach this level of consciousness. Heaven and hell are not externalised abstract destinations or God created. These energies exist here in everyday life, just look around you, observe the evening news and you will have your evidence right now. We create our heavenly or hellish experiences through our consciousness. Where you incarnate is determined by the spiritual work you have done on your-self in this and every lifetime. Shifting your consciousness will impact on the quality of this life and every life that you live. Becoming aware and living with awareness positively impacts on all life, providing meaningful purpose and benefits for everyone and everything. Imagine a time of pure beauty, living lovingly as one, sharing sustainably with all beings in harmony and at peace.

Where you place your thoughts is a choice whether you are positive or not. This is your consciousness. If you are operating out of sub-conscious programming, habit, pattern, pain or practice, this is your consciousness. For you to change, you need to take total responsibility for what you are feeling, where you place your mind, where you focus, what you say and how you act. This sounds like hard work although it is not. All you have to do is catch your thoughts in the process of building their stories, the justifications and reasons for being. If these thoughts are producing positive loving results for you then follow this infinite energy on its course. If your life is not working out, then just maybe it is time for you to make some changes. It really is up to you to make a difference in your life.

Love—My truth exists in the true loving feelings expressed through my thoughts, words and actions in every moment.

FLOW OF POSITIVE ENERGY

Your ability to create the flow of positive, loving energy in every aspect of your life is determined by your consciousness. Your awareness of any negative, restrictive, fearful patterns and programs and your ability to transmute these physical limitations illustrates your consciousness. To be able to set your-self free to experience all of your life requires you to release all doubt, all fear, all negative thoughts and behaviours and any other energy that restricts the flow of your life and sharing of your love. Love is pure liberation, setting you free to be all of your-self. When you are in a loving space, you will be free and responsible to be all of who you really are. You are always supported and enhanced by the energy around you.

Traditional social conditioning and repetitious physical experience solidifies and convinces us that our current lifestyle is the best it can be or is it? Do you really feel that you are at the peak of your powers and that we are making the best use of the magnificent resources our beautiful planet has to offer? I know that we are not and that it has been eons since we have been sensitive to the inner needs of ourselves, of others or the planet. Cultures that are still in tune with the earth and living as nature intended are far more advanced in this regard than our so called civilised world. We have been very effective in building out nature, disconnecting ourselves from the earth and treating our life force with distain and disregard. I cannot believe nor accept that this is the best we can do with all the resourcefulness, inventiveness and universal intelligence we have available to us.

Each of us has responsibility to do what we can in our lives to positively influence our lives and any other life that invites us to share our energy. Avoiding or neglecting this responsibility only hurts ourselves and delays the inevitable consequences of unsustainable negative energy. Only love and positivity are eternally sustainable for these prime energies nurture and foster real peace to create harmony and balance within the universe. Do what you are inspired to create positive loving energy in every aspect of your life and you will be pleasantly and constantly amazed with your own power. You are the source of your own creation, accept this responsibility and flourish as the magnificent being of light that you are.

Love—I am positive loving energy in all my creation reflected in all my thoughts, words and deeds.

JUST BE

You are a human being, not a human doing. Take a moment and allow your-self to just be. Take a break from all external distractions, family, work or business, the constant activity trap and relentless doing that controls your life. The only reality you ever experience is inside of you in each precious moment. When you are too busy to notice that life seems to be flashing by, you need to bring your-self back to your speed of life. Our greatest challenge in life is within ourselves and finding real meaning for our existence. Regardless of how much physical effort we expend in looking outside of ourselves, our results at best will be superficial and temporary. All of physical life is fleetingly impermanent, life and death comes to all things, passing from one existence to another rapidly continues through eternity. What you physically create and achieve can only last for only one lifetime. What you create spiritually or energetically will serve you and the universe forever.

This primary question of life should be the sole motivation and intention for all our creations and it can only start within your-self. Someone else is not able to do it for you nor can they make it better for you. If anything is going to be, it really is up to you to do it. Be in each moment to allow your-self to just be. Be quiet, still and at ease within your mind. This stillness will enable you to receive the soft, gentle guidance and wisdom of your soul. If you wish to learn how to be, venture into nature and observe how nature is. Nature is not constantly busy doing lots of things over and over again, not competing or confronting unnecessarily, not in a hurry, not acquiring nor grasping, not damaging or destroying itself nor is it jealous or envious of its neighbours. Nature just holds its consciousness in its space, observing, being and sharing its energy freely and lovingly with all who wish to feel her energy. Spend time in nature within your-self and feel how nature feels, feel how all time and space exists only in the now.

Just being who you are is your natural state. You are not separate from nature, the planet or the universe. Connect with the very being of your essence, your spirit and you will know why you exist and why you have created this life for you. Whenever you feel disconnected, conflicted or confused, be as nature is and feel your life force pulsating infinitely within you and you will know what you need to create next. You will always know what is right for you. Just be with the pure feelings of your truth and you will know. Come back to your-self, allow your-self to be and let your life energy flow freely.

Love—I am a spiritual human being in this moment.

FUN AND JOY

The essence of your spirit is child-like—free, loving, fun, joyful, imaginative, creative, in the moment, self focussed, innocent, accepting and beautiful. This is who you really are. You have not grown out of your child-self; you have just grown around this beautiful essence while trying to be all grown-up. I have always felt to grow-up is to stop growing. You may catch glimpses of your child-self in those moments where you feel free to let your guard down, be silly and be your-self. In those rare moments when you are really present, you can let your hair down and frolic, skip and play, create and daydream without a care in the world. This is when you feel at your best and grateful for all of your life. You have not forgotten your child self, you just trained your-self to think your way through life instead of really feeling your way.

When you come back to your child-self, you will know you. For too long we have all tried hard to be far too earnest and serious about life only to find that we are all playing the same grown-up game of make believe with dire consequences. With time and experience you will find that everyone is doing the same thing, playing their respective roles to the best of their ability. Most of the fun and joy seem missing in these lives, never mind any sense of happiness or fulfilment. If you are still subscribing to the paradigm of doing, acquiring and possessing to be content this will be your reality. It will only be when you have over achieved that you may realise that this was not real at all and can disappear in a flash. There will be a time in your life when your core beliefs are really tested and you will know that there is more to life than what you do and your station in life. When you have this breakthrough, your child—self will have some answers for you.

Come back to your child to find that memory of when you last felt free to be your-self without being concerned about how you look or what others think of you. When you come back to your child, you will no longer wish to punish or abuse this child by distracting, stupefying or distorting your—self with artificial or chemical substances that do not honour nor serve your body. You would not feed drugs, alcohol or cigarettes to a child no more than you should ingest these substances in your body or spirit. Think about this concept and ask your-self, are you really loving and nurturing your soul by treating you in this way. Having real love for your-self is reflected in how well you love and treat you in every circumstance.

You are free to play freely, doodle, fiddle, day dream, dance, sing, laugh, chant, twirl, ride, swim, run, skip, create, lay, sleep, bask, scribble and rant just as you did when you were a child. When you are this free, you will know exactly what makes your heart spirit soar and smile with all the knowing of the universe that you require in each moment. Set your-self free from all your adult shackles and reservations and you will begin again to know and accept who you have always been. Try it, you will have real fun and find your life joyfully magical again.

Love—I am my child-self and play freely and creatively.

SIMPLICITY

Simplicity is the truth of your spirituality. When you come back to the essence of who you are, you will realise that the core of all life is in its simplicity. Everything in all existence is energy, vibrating to establish the reality in which you find your-self. When you strip life down to its basic elements, you will find the simple ease of its flow. In our insatiable quest to improve our quality of life and the acquisition of greater physical value, we are encouraged to be well educated, intellectual and well connected socially. To be successful, respected, loved, intelligent, wealthy, famous and heroic are common human aspirations. We believe that when we have all that we materially desire that we will be somebody or something. When you ascend your mountain of success, is the view any prettier or do you just see all the bodies and souls you have climbed over to achieve your goals? The truth is, regardless of what you possess or who you think you are, if you have ignored your spirit and its desires along the way, you will always be missing something in your life.

Your spirit is simple, it is totally connected to all life and the universe, its truth is compassionate, considerate and caring and it wants what is best for all life and not just for itself. When you are coming from your spiritual core you will know because you will be in total resonance with your soul. It will feel right on every level within you, in your heart, in your mind, in your body, within your soul. This is not a program, it is you and you will know the difference. Come back to who you really are and you will know what you need to create in every moment.

Whenever you have a question, quietly and respectfully ask your spirit for the answer and then listen patiently for the answer. At first you may just receive a hint, one word or a whisper of an answer for you are still learning to listen to your spirit. With patience, persistence and practice you will start to hear your truth quite clearly. You will know it is your truth as it will always be simple, easy, positive, loving, nurturing and honouring for you. At times you will be conflicted by your answers as they may involve or affect others. This can be challenging however just remember that you are only responsible for your-self and your actions. In receiving guidance, you need to look for the intended meaning of the parable or metaphor that you have been provided. While spirit is simple, it is not direct nor literal as this would remove your power of choice. You will receive guidance to move you, not to direct you.

We all need to come back to the simplicity and joy of life to start really embracing all of life on this planet. Be your-self within the planet and you will feel all the universe flowing beautifully through you in all that you are.

Love—Keep It Simple Spirit.

JOURNEY WITHIN

The only truth you will ever truly know will be the truth that lies deep within your soul's memory. When you spend real time getting to know who you really are, you will start to gain access to your cellular memory which is always connected to universal consciousness. Connect with your essence and you will know. This universal knowing is far more powerful than your physical intelligence can ever be programmed to be. What you can actually think will always be limited and mutable. What you feel is infinite and cannot be programmed or categorised. Your true feelings are your truth. What you feel is unique to you. Your feelings have been cultivated and nurtured through numerous lifetimes and experiences in many forms. Your feelings are not limited by beliefs, rituals or rules. They just are what they are and should not to be confused with your emotions. Your emotions are generally your programmed reactions to your circumstances based on past experiences, training, wounds, patterns and beliefs held within the mind.

Your feelings are those miniscule senses you receive deep inside you just before you actually start to think or react to each experience. Your feelings are subtle and obscure as you are not used to feeling them. In fact, during most of our lives we have actively resisted and fought our natural feelings as they have not told us what we wanted to hear. How many times have you felt something and pushed it down, ignored it or dismissed it as an impossibility only to find later that they were accurate. What is often regarded as gut feelings are your true feelings and these strong feelings exist in all of us regardless of gender. Unfortunately all of our society is being masculinised, encouraged to believe that only the mind has worthwhile intelligence. Even the feminine movement of the 60s turned out to be a masculine movement as women became more like men. The intuitive feminine energy will always be far more powerful than masculine intelligence and these vital feminine qualities should have been encouraged, not squandered. If our intelligence is superior, why has the quality and meaningful purpose of all lives on this planet not improved substantially given all the resources and so-called technological advances we have available to us.

As we have become apparently more civilised and sophisticated it would seem that we have lost touch with ourselves, each other and with this magnificent planet that sustains us. Given the might of our intelligence, we should have our greatest people leading and inspiring us, ensuring the needs of everyone were cared for and that we lived and loved sustainably and wholly. It is unfortunate that this is not the case although therein lies an opportunity for all of us. We are a diverse and multi—talented species capable of enormous potential if only we accepted and realised that we all have an important and essential role to play in this world together. We are all part of the whole, connected at the soul with all existence, eternal and all knowing and nothing is stopping us being this potential. Listen to your-self, to your inner wisdom and follow your own guidance. You do know.

Love—I am a being of supreme universal intelligence connected to all existence.

COMPASSION

Compassion for your-self and others is one of the greatest acts of kindness you can offer humanity and the environment. Through being considerate and caring of your-self, you set the standard of compassion in all of your life. How you think and treat your-self in every way reflects itself in all your experiences and your relationships with others. Generally we are misguided in believing that others will treat us as we treat them. As it is not possible to give an energy that you have not yet experienced, it is also not possible to receive this same energy if you have no feeling or sense of it. Therefore it is essential that you treat your-self as you would like the world to treat you and observe your whole experience of reality change.

Compassion will be evident in all that you are. Your feelings, how you think, how you express your-self and definitely how you act will become more loving and honouring in all of your life. A 15 year old once explained to me this was the very notion of karma. If you have negative thoughts, words and acts, these are the disabling, destructive energies you release into your reality and this can be the only energy that returns to you. The amplification of this negativity will be generated through your level of joy and pleasure you have with this experience. This also applies even more powerfully to the release of positive, loving thoughts, words and acts as these are enabling supportive energies that enhance the evolution of everyone.

With the complete acceptance of the pure loving spiritual being that you are, you will be more aware of your feelings and how your mind interprets the world around you. You will be conscious of where you place your mind, how critical, judgemental, negative, loving, considerate, accepting and compassionate that you are in every circumstance. Our mind is processing information from all around us, from within us, assimilating, categorising and comparing experiences with the past, present and future many millions of times a day. Bring your-self back to each moment, feel how you feel in this moment, then use the power of your mind to enable the will of your spirit. Let go of all negative self talk, release all fears no matter how small and allow your-self to be free to be all of you. Compassion will release and enable your spirit.

Love—I am compassionate with my-self and all others.

OPEN YOUR HEART

Inside all beings is an enormous beating heart full of pure and complete love that few of us ever get to truly experience as we often seek this love outside of ourselves. The energy of true love exists inside every being on this planet, yet why do we find it so hard to find, enhance and sustain real love in our lives. This is one of the essential energies of life that can only be felt from within your-self. Love is not a tangible energy or commodity that can be given to you from another. Others can show you love, share their love with you, treat you with love and even give you love, but is this really love? Love is often described as an energy you receive from another or is given to you from outside of your-self. Your experience of love will always be hard to actually describe or define and so it should be. Love is your divine expression and will always be highly individual and unique. Love is pure energy, it emanates from within your very core, it is the vital manifestation of our soul's energy, it is who you are and what you are about.

When you really open your heart to the flow of your love you will know the difference. You will know and accept this vital essence of your-self and this will be the energy that manifests and sustains everything you do. Spend the time to really get to know every aspect of your-self just as you would when you get to know another. Discover what inspires or limits you, turns you on and off, enhances and motivates you, serves and honours you, feels right and good and what doesn't. You will soon begin to know you in every way and be okay with who you are and who you wish to be. Accept all the light, shade, dark and in between all of you and you will know love. Your love of you will be whole and complete and this is the love you will share with all life.

Living with the flow of love in your heart will feel so right to you that you will wonder how or why you ever lived any other way. You will awaken to enjoy all that life has to offer you, feel and see with higher senses, observe without judgement, consider with compassion and you will desire what is best for everyone. With real love of your-self, you are never alone as you know that you exist in the greater love body of all spirit and know that as you are, all will be. Love emanates from within each of us, it is the source code of all that we are and all we were ever meant to be. When you know your love and live this love in every way, loving others is really just loving your-self. You cannot ever love your-self too much and as you love another is really your love of your-self overflowing through you to them. All energy flows through you, not from you and self-love should not be mistaken for ego or narcissism. With true love of you in your heart, you will not abuse, misuse, maltreat, criticise, stupefy, poison, neglect, downplay, judge or sadden your-self ever again.

Love—I love my-self in every moment.

RECEIVING HEART

When you open your heart to the flow of your love, you will find that your heart will open to be able to receive love. You can only acknowledge and receive energy that you have experienced within your-self. If you have not felt real love within you, it is really difficult to truly accept external love for you will have little understanding of this love. Generally we seek love from around us and neglect to look for this same love from its source within ourselves. Regardless of who or where you are, you have access to the infinite energy of universal love inside of you and all you have to do is accept this as your truth. Open your heart to all the possibilities of your-self and feel the full potential of your love's energy.

Energy in all its forms attracts what is familiar and known and repels what it does not recognise or know. For example, if you desire great, everlasting love in your life and you have not felt this level of love within you, you will not receive this love until you learn to really love your-self in this way. You will only receive higher energies or knowing when you change your vibration of love from within your-self. To be able to receive real love, you must first be the real love you desire. This is also true of all other forms of energy you wish to manifest in your life. Be the energetic change you wish to be. When you really open your heart and allow your-self to be highly sensitive and vulnerable, you allow your-self to feel and receive all the beauty and miracles the universe has to share. The truth of your love is in your sensitivity.

With an open heart you will be more sensitive than you have ever been and feel far more than you think you can handle. Always remember, there is no experience that you cannot handle and your soul will never set you up to fail. Your inner strength and fortitude has brought you to this point in your journey and I am sure that it has not all been a smooth ride. It never is for the inquisitive ones. Use your sensitivity and wisdom to observe life to form your own unique perspective without being consumed by the drama, negativity and fear mongering that prevails. You will not be controlled, subdued or manipulated ever again for you will not give your power away to anyone or anything. With an open heart, you will know what is true for you and you will really know how you need to live your life with focus and loving intention. It is your love that will enable and enhance your life and always remain open to and flowing with your infinite possibilities.

Love—I am love, open and free to receive all the abundance of the universe.

SELF RESPONSIBILITY

Being able to take total responsibility for your-self and your creativity is one of the greatest energetic enablers of the universe. When you take full responsibility for your-self, you take back your power to create your life the way you desire it to be. When you forgo this power, you remain servitude, emotional, victimised, needy and any other reservations you have imposed on your-self. Giving away your responsibility or taking responsibility for others also restricts the flow of your energy between the spiritual and physical worlds. Your spirit will always conserve your core energy ensuring you do not give your-self away completely. This restriction will make it extremely difficult to integrate these two inter-dependant energies. We have all spent many lifetimes of service, following others, programmed in one way or another, always looking for the next best thing, putting the needs of others before ourselves and so on. It is time to take back your responsibility for your creation of life and to be responsible for all that you are. Self responsibility will set you free.

You are totally responsible for all of your-self, how you feel, where you find your-self and your life circumstances. If you are seeking to change any aspect of your life, it is only you that can change you and only you live with the full consequences of your choices in this and every lifetime. Unfortunately if you are still in survival mode or really struggling with your creation of this life, then this concept is going to sound absurdly unacceptable, maybe even unspiritual. We do need to help those less fortunate than ourselves although I still suggest that you need to know how you are helping your-self or you may just miss your learning in the process. We are all here on earth to improve the quality of our lives through spiritual evolution. It is important for any culture that may be stuck in the endless power based cycle of violence, poverty, abuse, neglect, control, inequity, hedonism, consumption and materialism to find their way back to their spiritual core. As soul groups we become fanatical and obsessed with our dramatic patterning. We reincarnate repetitively into particular cultures, tribes or countries (possibly even changing sides) until we take personal responsibility for finding new loving solutions to resolve our petty historical, political and religious differences. This process takes as long as it takes.

Throughout the various stages in our incarnations, we have cleared many patterns to find ourselves with the freedom and resources to consider these new philosophies for living. It is also true that regardless of your social, environmental or political circumstances, each soul has the potential to rise from the ashes to magnificence with just one choice. When you take responsibility for all of your life you take control over how you live and you open to the full flow of universal energy through you. You will breathe in life fully. Allow your heart to expand enormously. Align your heart's love and head's intelligence to work together to improve your life and the lives of the souls you touch. Being responsible is neither burdensome nor onerous. It is liberating and enabling for you now have the power to be all of who you desire to be.

Love—I am totally responsible for all I create, experience and live.

QUIETEN THE MIND

Awareness of your mind's focus is a precious gift. Many of us practice meditation, mind control techniques, psychology, exercise or other methods of understanding the workings of the mind. All I know is the mind never sleeps, never shuts up and always has something to say about everything. Always thinking, judging, critiquing, analysing, sorting, processing and on it goes always chattering away. We have become such an intellectual society always on the move, busy acquiring whatever we want, online, on the phone, socialising or through many other forms of distraction. If we are not busy than something must be amiss and please do not ever be alone with your-self. You might feel something that you do not know what to do with and then who will you be if you are not busy. Sound familiar. We have all fallen into this busyness trap at some stage and it is interesting that even spiritual beings revert to old habits if the circumstances re-present. Our learning is constant.

Finding your way to quieten your mind is a very personal thing and you will try many methods before you find what works for you. All I know is that you need to find your way to still your mind to be able to listen to your heart, to access your feelings. When the mind is busy, regurgitating the past, planning for the future, thinking about everything and everyone, it cannot possibly focus on your-self or what you are feeling. Your mind is incredibly important to you, to your health and just about everything you do. It is not your enemy, but it is also not your friend otherwise it would have looked after you much better than it has. Your mind's soul purpose is to enable your feelings and it will achieve this when it is out of the way.

When you can quieten your mind by letting go of needing to know everything, you will start to feel for your truth. Your true feelings will feel right for you, will honour you and love you. Your feelings are your truth and you will know when you have accessed them. Like all universal truth, you will only know when you know your feelings and you cannot know before you do. I know that my truth always loves and honours my journey and when I truly listen to my feelings, my path flows smoothly and when I ignore my-self, I pay the price. Simply come back to what you know, listen without judgement or analysis and act attentively with trust and observe any changes in your results. Be patient and trust your process as it can take time for your energies to re-align themselves to your path, it will happen. Once you have accessed your true feelings, use the power of your mind to enable you to create your dreams and desires. With your head and heart combined you will achieve real greatness.

Love—My feelings are my truth and I am committed to living my truth.

LEARNING FOCUS

Every experience, each lifetime, each incarnation serves our evolution when we understand the purpose for our lives. Just as in life, as we learn, hopefully we grow although this is not always the case. With greater information and greater knowing, you will know how much we still have to learn. From my perspective I do not feel that we can intellectually comprehend the infiniteness of the universe, nor is it necessary for all of us to know all there is to know. I feel that each of us is here for a unique purpose and when we understand more about ourselves, we will know why we are here and this has been my experience. While we may only be small particles of energy in all space, each of us has a role to play and it is important that we play it.

When you piece together all of your life, reflecting on all the skills, attributes or information you have created, you will find that you have designed your life in your own fashion and you will not be like anyone else. You will be uniquely you. Now consider that you have journeyed through numerous lifetimes and in each lifetime gone through a similar process, all cumulating to who you are right now. The energy that has developed and sustained you to this point has been forged and shaped by your unique experiences and skills you have developed in each lifetime. Therefore you are very unique and isn't it time for you to let your-self be free.

You are committed to being free to love all of who you are and you will achieve this hearty goal by letting go of everything that is not who you really are. You will identify and dissipate all negative, fearful, judgemental, critical and non-believing energies that restrict, limit and sabotage your evolution. Look at all your fears, no matter how miniscule they appear and see them for what they are. If you are not currently facing a dangerous situation, your fears will not be real nor do they have any real substance. Look at your fears where you are right now and consider whether these thoughts serve you in this moment or are they just a reflection of past wounds, experiences or traumas. If your fears are not real in this moment, they do not serve any purpose, so let them go. Find a new point of focus that does serve and honour you. You will always find your answers in the positive, loving energies that enable you to be responsible for changing your perspective, memory, thoughts, actions and dreams. There will always be a positive answer for you and sometimes this will impact on others, however they too are responsible for their learning. Be conscious of your-self and of the experiences you have created for your growth and you will really begin to receive the purposeful gift of your life.

Love—Everything in my life guides and teaches me more about my-self.

LOVING RELATIONSHIPS

Throughout our lives we have a myriad of relationships with other people whether they are with family, romantic, friendships, associates or work mates. Generally these relationships influence and determine the opinion we have of ourselves. Unless you live cocooned in isolation as a hermit, you will have connections and interactions with people of all persuasions, cultures, beliefs and consciousness. There is no avoiding this reality and why would you want to when these relationships form a significant portion of your evolution. It is one thing to spend time getting to know your-self in isolation however you will never know how conscious you really are until you share the light of your awareness publicly. Being able to stand in your truth when most people will not understand or accept where you are coming from requires real courage and belief in who you really are.

Living your consciousness requires you to live the love of your truth in all circumstances and regardless of where you find your-self. As the great Buddha shared, "before enlightenment, carrying water and chopping wood. After enlightenment, carrying water and chopping wood". You will not necessarily change what you are doing, however you will be more conscious in the doing. This is also true of your relationships. It is not necessary to change or end some or all of your relationships just because you wish to find your-self and have a real relationship with your-self. This process can be done in conjunction with all other aspects of your life and you have all the time in the world to get to know your-self. You are not going anywhere where you will not be present. So take the time and make the effort to get to know and understand all of your-self and you will know how beautiful and complete you already are.

For too long we have been convinced that we are what other people think of us and how they treat us. This could not be further from the truth. What we think can only be sourced from within ourselves and our consciousness will be reflected in our opinions of others. These opinions and judgements will be limited by our experiences, knowledge and knowing and upon how loving, conscious and compassionate we are or not. Generally our judgements reflect only what we know of a past experience or drama and do not represent our current situation. Therefore why are we basing so much emphasis on what others say, their opinions, fears, insecurities, judgements, stereotypes, archetypes, categorising, cultural behaviours and programmed belief or thought control systems. We subscribe to group thinking to fit in and to make sense of a life that does not seem to make any sense at all. We just do not know any better. Anyone who questions life tends to find many more questions than answers and sometimes wonder why they bother. A great teacher and friend once advised me that you better be sure in opening the door to your soul for as you become more conscious, you cannot consciously become unconscious again.

Love—I love all that I am and I share my love freely and responsibly.

LIFE'S LESSONS

Every experience you have gone through in this lifetime has shaped, influenced, guided and led you right to this moment. The fact that you are right here is a reflection of the lessons of life that you have received at some level whether you were aware of them or not. Take out one moment, one experience, even one drama and you would be elsewhere, considering other aspects of your life. It doesn't take more than a simple choice to completely change your life, your educational subjects, work or profession, your relationships, sporting or creative interests, unsatisfied desires or dreams or as basic as turning left instead of right. It can be and is that simple. Who you are today reflects all of these choices collectively building to this moment and indicates the perfection of the process of your evolution.

You need to acknowledge the courage and strength you have within you to prosper beyond everything you have experienced and know that you have the ability to fearlessly face all the life lessons that you can create. Once you know that you cannot be really hurt or damaged, you will stand with true strength of spirit in all that you face. Know that most of our emotional fears are paper thin, they are fictional and easy to walk through when we know this to be possible. We often fear what we do not or cannot know. This is not dismissing that pain is real, that there are real life traumas and that some stories are so sad or horrid. These situations are true and valid. However you still choose whether you wish to live forever consumed by this trauma and overwhelmed. Your sad story, depression, trauma and wounds should not rule and destroy the rest of your life, nor should they ruin the lives of those you love. Hard as this may be to accept, there is a time for grieving and regret however there comes a time when the past needs to be left exactly where it was. Learn your life lessons. Understand there are no accidental or chance events. Everything we create is here for us to learn and grow from. When you can accept this, you will begin to dig your-self out of whatever deep dark hole you have dug for your-self. Some of us seem comfortable and content with being habitually sad and upset. You will not be motivated to make any effort to change until you realise there is more to life than being miserable, sad, upset, depressed and wounded all the time. Life is meant to be fun, interesting, joyful and full of love. Is this your experience and would you like it to be.

When you are ready to accept that you can re-create your life with one new choice, you will be ready to learn and grow and you will know how clever and brave you really are. Consider for a moment you are the creator of your reality and just maybe you did powerfully create whatever wound you are afflicted with your own fears or negativity. When you switch to creating from a more loving positive base, imagine how powerful you really are when you have the universe on your side. Work with your spirit in all you are, sustaining you in your moments of doubt and weakness and ensuring that you will prevail no matter what. You are more powerful and wise than you can imagine, just stay out of your way and allow the energy of your spirit to show you the way. Who you are is not your pain or wound. Who you are is loving, vital, wise, knowing and energetic in every way.

Love—I accept the lessons of my life and I evolve in my learning.

RELEASE ALL PAIN

Just with all our experiences, pain or wounds created as a result of an event are here to remind us of who we are not meant to be. When you honestly reflect on your life, you will admit there were many times when you did not listen to your inner voice of wisdom, times when this voice was screaming at you to change directions or make a different choice. With the benefit of hindsight, you are able to acknowledge that maybe you should have listened and things may have been otherwise. This may be so however you can only be aware of your options when you become more aware of you and how clear you are in creating your life. Our spirit and physical bodies are talking to us all the time through hints, inklings, gut feelings, senses and sometimes even more obvious guidance only to be ignored, put off or dismissed. It does not really matter when or how we get our messages, it just matters that we eventually wake up.

The pain in our bodies is the manifestation of many lifetimes of ignorance, abuse, neglect or just plain bloody mindedness. Whatever discord, disease and injuries we create within ourselves remains within our psychic memories regardless of whether we physically heal these ailments or not in each lifetime. All disease emanates from this soul memory to be re-created in each lifetime until we acknowledge, accept and resolve whatever energy created this discord in the first instance. You do not need to go back through every lifetime to re-discover the cause. Deal with whatever issues you have created in this lifetime and you will clear this discordant energy within you and through all time and space. To return to who we really are, we need to work through whatever is presenting in our way, understand our role in its creation and our gifts in being able to resolve and clear this energy. Unfortunately this seems to be the process we have created to integrate into these physical bodies and to be able to fully live our spirits in this human form.

You will know your process to heal your-self. All you have to do is to remember who you are, give your-self permission to let go of anything that is not aligned to your spirit. Find your process to clear this discordant energy and any other energy that does not serve your soul's purpose. We all have the ability to heal ourselves if only we accept we are of the universe, infinitely powerful and capable of all the universe has to offer. This is real power not to be mis-used or abused. It is there to be used for good loving intent. Any attempts to use this power inappropriately or with negative intent will only serve to amplify the journey of the soul involved. We have all seen the mis-use of power and the harm it creates. Ensure that you do not need to fear or feed this drama through your own positive, loving and clear intent.

Love—I love my pain and I listen and act upon its guidance.

ACCEPT TO FORGIVE

Acceptance is the powerful key to forgiveness. When you are able to accept your role in the creation of all your experiences, you will begin the process of letting go of all negative, fearful energies that restrict and inhibit your evolution. With true acceptance in your heart, you have shown the strength of character and spirit to come through your experiences with your soul intact. Acceptance sets you free. In accepting life, its challenges and achievements, its heavenly and hellish, its positive and negative, you will clearly observe how you have evolved. You will know that you have experienced what you have needed to go through to be who you are today. While you were responsible, you will also know that you or no-one else was to blame. We can only do the best we know with the knowledge and energy that is running through us at that time. If you knew more, had clearer information available and were able to feel your way, it is likely your circumstances may have been different but this is often not the case. I do not believe that anyone of us awakens each morning with plans to ruin our day, however how many times does this happen before we realise that it is only ourselves creating our own mess. We have far more power and deserve to create real magic and beauty in our lives.

Shift may happen to you in a huge way. Life may have dealt you some disastrous cards. You may have been borne to the wrong family, in the wrong place at the wrong time. Unfortunately this is not possible, you have created this incarnation exactly as you intended to fully comprehend and accept your spirit and all you need to know inside of you. Your consciousness, your vibration determines each life you live. Your experiences, both positive and negative will continue to create your vibration through all eternity. When we persistently deny the truth of who we are, we create experiences that will dramatically and traumatically push us back onto our paths. Your experiences shape you into the magnificent being that you are and you know that nothing can break your spirit.

It is with true knowing of your spirit that you accept your past in this and every life. You will accept your role in creating your life and you will forgive your-self and everyone else involved. With acceptance and forgiveness you will free your-self of the past, you will release any painful, harmful memories and you will sever any negative karma you may have created with other souls. Acceptance is incredibly powerful and allows you to move on with your life. It draws a line in the sand saying, no more. I am not succumbing to my fears or negativity. I am taking my power back from my wounds and I am now creating lovingly and positively in all of my life. Whenever you create or observe negativity in any of its forms, just accept its presence without judgement, seek a positive alternative and remain loving to you. You are here to love and be loved. Allow your-self to create with love and accept all the beautiful pure energy that you are.

Love—I accept the power of all my creations and release all energy with love.

CLEARING NEGATIVE ENERGY

Everything is energy, light and dark, positive and negative, love and fear, all balanced and evolving perfection. It is when these energies are out of balance is when we need to intervene. If fear and negativity are dominating your life and you cannot find any positives in the darkness, you need to be able to clear your way back to your light. This starts with your seed intention. You will have recognised a need to change and accepted your role in being this change. No-one else can do your work for you. Be honest with your-self and review any role you may have played in creating your current or past circumstances. When you can see your contribution, reflect on your behaviours, habits or patterns and imagine how you would or could have done things differently. If you cannot find wisdom, ask for help and guidance from spirit, your supreme being or the universe. Being able to find positive loving alternatives is a skill you will develop with your consciousness. You may learn some skills from others, through experience or from your-self, it is just important that you learn how to live from a loving, positive perspective.

Being loving and positive in all elements of your life will clear your way back to you. Love clears all your fears. Just try loving you and others will naturally receive the gift of your love. When you create fearfully you are already limited by this destructive energy. Try giving love an opportunity to present its beautiful energy and watch your-self flourish. Love is the antidote to anything that is not flowing or working in your life and is definitely the answer to any negativity or fear. Our fears are often minor and non life threatening. They present in every day events as doubt, insecurity, regret, guilt, anguish, sorrow and any other negative emotional limitation you can imagine. When you find your-self in a non-loving fearful space, take the time to feel what is true and responsible for your-self and you will find your loving answer. In doing this you will clear your fears, you will no longer react to your circumstances and find your loving responses to whatever situation you are in.

Responding to life as it happens, observing life in its present form and receiving your guidance in each moment is being in the beautiful flow of your life. Let go of all restrictions and self imposed limitations to set your-self free to be all of your-self. Free your-self, love and be the best love you can be to re-ignite your light.

Love—I am clear of all negativity and fear.

INTUITION

Your inner connection to all universal knowing is your intuition. Every being on this planet has the ability to tune into themselves to access their inner feelings of pure light, love and truth. The inner voice of your intuition, communicates through those subtle gut feelings and soul whispers you receive in the moments just before you start to think your-self away from these feelings. How many times have you known that you have not made the choice that best honours your-self in order to fit in or belong? The truth is that none of us really fit inside these heavy, fearful, cumbersome and negatively ridden physical bodies and we spend so much time and energy trying so hard to fit. Who you are is pure spirit, light, loving, honest, simple, compassionate and connected. Imagine how you can be this being and be able to live honestly and lovingly no matter where you are. In this world we have become so disconnected from ourselves and each other that we have lost sight of what is real, spending all our energy perpetuating this illusion of life.

The inner knowing that exists inside your intuition is the truth of who you are and is connected all the energetic knowing of all universal existence through time and space. If this sounds too daunting or unimaginable, just allow your-self to accept that you have the answers that are right for your-self. Take the time to tune in, create a sacred space to listen and empty your mind totally to enable your-self to hear you. It will take some time and practice to hear your spirit for you may not yet be attuned to its vibration. With trust and patience, you will begin to hear the soft whispers of your soul. It may start with a word, an idea, colour, sound or a sense. It does not matter how it presents as long as you hear it. Remember that spirit is not literal or direct. Spirit communicates by parables, ideas, visions or metaphors to enable your power of interpretation and free will. It is your responsibility to feel out your truth and to enact the feeling of your message. The key to your intuition lies within your choices and your ability to take action with what you know.

Your intuition is the gift of your spirit. We all have this gift, some may be more in tune than others however we are all equally capable and powerful in our own right. Do not fear or restrict any aspect of your knowing. Your past has brought you here however it is not your present and will definitely not create your desired future. Remember that all guidance you receive will be for your-self as well as others and that you are required to actualise your spirit in this human form. Be in this moment, face your truth now and act always from your heart space to let your magical, spiritual life flourish.

Love—I listen to my feelings and always act upon my inner voice of wisdom.

WISDOM

Your soul has infinite access to all the energy and wisdom the universe has to offer. We often feel that only the especially talented ones receive the bountiful gifts of spirit. However they are not different or any more special than you are. The only difference is that they have learnt to listen and follow their spiritual voice of wisdom. We are all intuitive, we are all spirit and we are all human. There is no separation other than in the point of view held by your mind. You have intuitive gifts and when you start really listening to your clear inner knowing, you will know your speciality of purpose. Every one of us is here for a reason. Spirit has never left anyone behind or neglected any soul seeking its way. It is our own denial of our spiritual essence that creates our separation and isolation from our soul's intention. There can be no valid reasons or excuses to hinder your access to spirit. There are still many cultures today who are far more connected to themselves, each other and the planet than our supposedly sophisticated civilisations can ever conceive.

These enlightened societies are not cashed up, materialistic, highly educated or well fed. Through their connection to all of life, they are thriving in some of the most basic and simple lives you can imagine. These cultures know why they are here and how to live in balance and harmony. The common thread is their connection to their spirit and this is their key point of differentiation with our western cultures.

In our civilisations, we are lead to believe in country, governance, religion and control where we are told what, when, how and why to do most things in our lives. These are not overt or obvious state run mechanisms, these controls exist in the margins of our beliefs, traditions, cultures, habits and rituals. Most of us do not even realise we have been controlled or programmed until we reach that break-through point where you start to really question the reality you have found yourself in. It is at this moment that you realise that you have fallen asleep at the wheel. Most of your beliefs and behaviours do not have any real substance or validity. Your achievements are not sustainable and your legacy has no eternal life force other than its physicality. There is more to life than this physical existence and it is your soul. When your soul energy is integrated with your physical life, all of your life will make sense and you will have the ability to positively contribute and make a real difference with your life.

You have the ability and the power to instigate real changes in your life. Feel for your truth, feel what is right and loving for all involved and then use the enormous power of your intelligence to enable the physical creation of your intuitive knowing. Your mind is powerful and is generally used inappropriately to restrict us rather than to liberate and create life anew. Tune into your own wisdom, find your own answers and start to make your own way through your life. Trust your-self and your knowing and it will work out. You have come to this stage in your life to be real. It is okay to be your-self.

Love—Every answer to every question I have is within my soul.

TRUST YOUR TRUTH

In accessing your truth you will clearly know every step of your way. This truth will develop and evolve as you move along your path providing greater insights and clarity about life and your contribution to all evolution. Each soul you touch, whenever you share your knowing, will be positively altered by your energy. It is not only the masterful and powerful who are able to move mountains, it is the small and meek amongst us going about their work quietly and humbly that achieve the most significant change. In the age of celebrity and hero worship we are being distracted by glamour, illusion and pretence masquerading as reality that has us fooled. Go about your truth quietly, sharing what you know with those who seek you out, accept that we are all unique with something of value to share and be aware of the impact of your life on your-self. You are the only being that you can really change and as such, your truth is really only true for you in this present moment. As you grow, so too will your perspective, experience and knowing. Establish a sound foundation for your life then get out of your own way to allow this energy to flourish and prosper. You do not require the acceptance, validation or approval of anyone else for you to live your truth and as long as you are doing no harm, you will be supported by all of spirit.

Standing in your truth regardless of where you are can be challenging and confronting, particularly for those around you. One day you will awaken, feeling different, feeling like a stranger to other souls in your life. Someone once said to me in reflecting upon my life "that I was on a train going flat out in one direction only to reach the life changing station, walk across the platform and catch the train going flat out in the opposite direction". This is how change will appear to most people who are not close to you and still believe that life is a continuum of interconnected random events. When you start to make informed choices of the soul, it will appear to be contrary to others who are not yet familiar or connected with the truth of their own spirit. You will know the spiritually aware through their energy field, the love and compassion they will freely share with you. Seek out souls who enhance you.

We all exist within the one body of the universe with the same access to all there is to know. It is not necessary for you to know it all or even be able to comprehend all existence as I feel that this capacity maybe beyond the physical mind. However if you can accept that you can access this knowing that you need at any time you wish simply by sitting with the question and allowing the answer to present itself. This can happen in an instant, at a later time or present in some other obscure form. If you ask your-self a question or seek an answer about life, you are obliged to find your wisdom. This is how it works and has always worked. On some level you have already used this process to educate your-self. The only real difference now is that you are feeling your way as opposed to intellectualising your wisdom. You can only feel your way to your truth. It is extremely difficult to think or indoctrinate your spirituality. The truth of your spirit exists in the pure feelings of your sensory body. Who you are is unique and special. Your truth does not reside in your mind even if you may think you are more intelligent than spirit.

Love—My truth is my truth.

HIGHER SELF

Your highest, greatest loving thoughts of your-self will be your Higher Self, the physical representation of spirit here on earth. This is the intention of all spirit striving to be the best form of physical life we can dream of being, supported and nurtured by all the resources of the universe. We have incarnated for this reason, to be all the love, light and truth we can physically be. As eternal souls we have been on this journey forever, continually seeking to be our truth here in this form on this ever evolving planet of the universe. We are not new or strangers to this intention of spirit and you can be assured that you may have come close to actualising your spirit in other lifetimes only to be seduced by the allure and power of physicality. I am confident that we will fulfil our spiritual purpose. We will find real enlightenment and be able to live the truth of our love and light, freely and abundantly on this planet. This may inspire you or not, that is your choice. All I know is that this intention lights the eternal flame in my soul.

Step into who you really are, accept all that you can be and be all that you were meant to be and observe all the opportunities of the universe open before your heart. Who you are is already a magnificently beautiful and powerful being of pure energy. All you have to do is accept all of your-self, follow the energy of your heart's desire and this will change your perspective. Be aware of your primary feelings, of where you place your mind, how you express your creativity and be loving in all your actions and you will find your higher self. Your higher self is your highest thought of your-self, it is the best you can be and more, it is the self you dream for your-self, it is all your possibilities and potential, your higher self is all of who you are in both physical and spiritual form. Allow your-self to imagine for a moment how your life would be when you decide to be who you are in all ways. Do not allow the doubting, cynical, untrusting, negative, fearful lower self to hold you down, distract or bully you into denying your-self. Make new choices that honour, serve and love you and you will re-create your life beautifully.

Life is meant to be easy, rewarding and joyous and through being who you are, you will achieve everlasting love and happiness in all of your life. Your higher self is who you are meant to be to create real meaning, purpose, commitment and contentment with all you manifest. You know your-self better than any other and it is time for you to be free to be all of your-self.

Love—I know all of who I am and I am my best self.

FOCUSED INTENTION

Everything in our reality is created through our intention whether you are conscious of the seeds you have sown or not. Our primary intention is the seed motivation for everything we create in either the positive or negative sense. The source intent derived from your first conscious feeling of a particular energy or desire will be where your energy flows. If your first thought is negative, regardless of how positively you wish to affirm away your own fears or negativity, all you are really doing is positively re-affirming this negativity. To be able to focus your intention, you need to be in clear communication with your inner wisdom through your pure loving feelings that are your intuition. You must be able to tell the difference between your conscious responses and your programmed reactions to life.

Invest your energy in getting to feel all of your senses and to be able to hear the guidance you have for you. When you come back to your-self and begin to remember why you are here, you will start to really know what you are about and have real purpose in all of your life. Listen in every moment to how you feel about where you are and the people you are with, your feelings will be filtering, discerning and clarifying the truth of all the energy all around you. Often these base or gut feelings are dismissed, ignored or critically judged by our intellectual desire to belong and be accepted by the group. However it is these feelings that are true for you keeping you firmly on your path. What is true of you is not necessarily true for others nor is it necessary for you to follow the path of others. Each of us has our own path and destiny to fulfil and it is important we follow our inspiration and guidance. Try loving and honouring your-self and experience how life honours you in return.

Through knowing and accepting your soul's purpose, you will come back to your truth and all your energy will be invested in the evolution of your spirit. This is why we are all here, all of us striving to follow the love in our heart (not always successfully and that too is okay) and attempting to live the best life we can. I do not believe that there is a soul incarnation that does not desire this destiny and none of this concerns our physical aspirations or achievements. Life is all about how we feel, how we are living, how involved and included we are in our communities and the peace, love and happiness we share and experience. That is a life well lived with love and it does not really matter how much you possess or consume. The only energy you will take with you is soul energy and it is wise to spend some energy focussed on clearing your soul. Even if our consideration of what we know to be spirit is another illusion we have created for our own sense of importance, if you clean up your life, repair all your relationships particularly with your-self and start living a more heart filled, loving and peaceful existence, the quality of your current life will naturally improve. Everything exists in the now. Live, love and be who you are right here, right now and observe your creation of magical bliss.

Love—I live my loving truth in every moment.

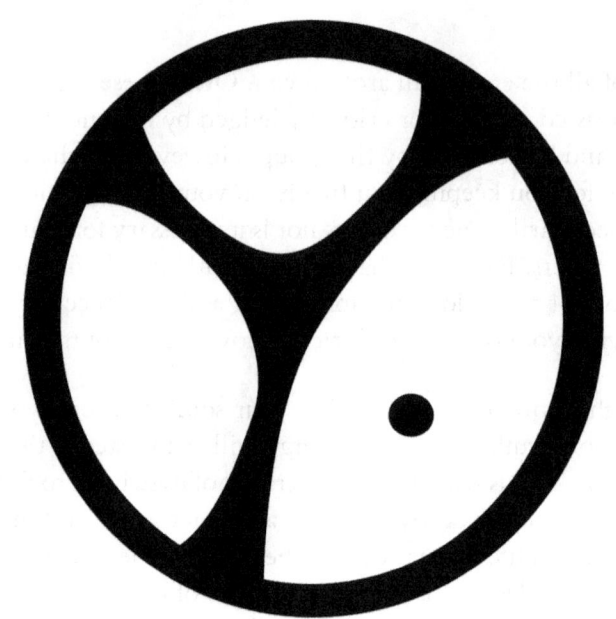

BE DISCERNING

Our pure loving feelings are the truth of who we really are and these senses are our connection to the infinite wisdom of the universe. Too often we dismiss or ignore our feelings as they are contrary to what we are thinking or the group view may be. The initial sense or feeling about situations, people or something is generally true and this will have been borne out in many of your experiences right through your life. The common definition of a feeling is a physical or emotional sense or instinctive notion. While this may be true on a physical level, your feelings are far more powerful and essential on the metaphysical level. Your feelings are highly developed and deeply connected even though you may be out of practice or out of tune. Your feelings are your energetic resonance with all the energies in the greater body of all existence through time and space. This may sound a little fanciful if you have not experienced or acknowledged your own intuitive abilities. However I can assure you that your infinite spiritual gifts and talents have far more to offer you than the finite physical world can ever hope to offer or provide.

Tuning into your core feelings in every moment will act as your receptor and barometer of the truth. To achieve this you will need to be fully grounded and present in every moment. While this may sound like an effort, it quite simply starts with setting your intention to be conscious and present. This intention activates your consciousness and you will be more aware of everything around you without necessarily having to be involved or concerned with having to correct anything. Your awareness will enable you to observe the perfection in the imperfection and know that everything and everyone is exactly where they need to be for their evolution. In every moment be aware of how you feel, know your truth of the situation and you will receive your insights. This will be your truth and when it feels right for you to follow, take action. If it does not feel right for you, then let it go for it is not meant for you. This is where your discernment is applied, your feelings will filter through all the useless or meaningless activity to find the real gems of guidance that will accelerate and amplify the truth of who you are.

Your feelings are not to be confused with your programmed emotions, impulsive reactions and attachments. Your feelings are far more advanced than these basic human traits. Your true feelings are always loving, honest, free, simple, easy and will always honour your journey even though on the surface they may not appear to honour others. Follow your feelings on the truth of your path and allow your-self to be free to be all of who you are.

Love—My pure feelings ignite my love.

ANSWERS TO LIFE

Through your intimate knowing of your true feelings you will have gained your access to all the wisdom of the universe. When you connect with your spiritual energy you will find the answers to all your questions. These answers may not come in a form that you are familiar with or even agree with initially. The answers will come and it will be for you to discern what information resonates with you and what doesn't. As with all energetic creations, it is your responsibility to take positive and loving action with this information. A useful tool to develop is your ability to know the difference between your self interest and the greater good to benefit all. One of the Buddhist's philosophies of "doing no harm" is of good use here. Should you apply this "no harm" approach in all of your life, including within your-self, you will find you will live differently, treating your-self and all others more lovingly. This approach starts with accepting love and positivity transmute all negative, fearful thoughts, how you express your-self, what you ingest in your body, where you live, work and play and in all other forms of thought, creativity and action you undertake.

You will receive new and different answers to all your questions. The real skill is to select the responses that will honour and serve your path and also how you share your experiences with others. Choosing this way of life often places you at odds with the general consensus within your community and you will need to tread lightly and consciously with those close to you. Nothing triggers hostility quicker than evangelistic new age preaching of the next coming of Christ. Always remember that everyone has their own way to realise in their own time. The fact that you have found your path does not mean necessarily that your way is appropriate for another. This also applies to my truth that I am sharing with you here. If you seek out or invite the truth then it will present for you. Just like all of life should be, the truth cannot be forced, organised, controlled, enlisted, restricted or manipulated in any way. When you really know you, you will know how you are meant to share your-self and what you know. In the meantime, just be loving to your-self and those around you and you will be sharing your experience of your truth. Walk in the light and your light will walk with you. If you happen to do no more than being your spirit on earth, you have achieved what you came here to do.

Love—I seek my answers through my connection with my-self, the earth and the universe.

RELEASE ANGER

Identify any negative, fearful energy that restricts and inhibits your life in any way. These energies create discord beyond our knowing not only in our bodies but through the greater body of all existence. Every seed of negativity we sow in our own bodies is germinated right through the universe and the contrary is also true, every positive seed produces accordingly. We do not realise the power of creation we all possess within our core and we do not utilise this energy effectively to re-create with positive loving intention. When we are negative, fearful, sick and in conflict, this is the energy we share with ourselves, each other and all life. It is accepted that life here can be painful, disturbing, harsh and at times absolutely brutal without obvious good reason. Everything we have or will ever create has purposeful intent and has been created for us to grow through, not to be stuck in. Humanity is obsessed with holding onto wounds, desperately hanging onto the insanity of bloody conflict, victimhood, criminality, injustice, winners and losers. I have never understood our blatant inability and unwillingness to live lovingly, peacefully and compassionately.

Real peace is derived from accepting the perfection of the imperfection that exists in all our creations now and through all time. We study the distortion and bias of history without seemingly being able to learn or grow from its lessons. Civilisations have repetitively come and gone from this planet without good reason other than they somehow missed the vital signs that they needed to change or adapt to their changing circumstances. We are currently in a similar situation where we are living in disharmony and unsustainably, consuming everything and everyone along the way. We seem fatalistic and existing selfishly for today with little regard for the souls that will inherit our legacy. We do need to change our ways and all this change starts within each one of us. If we wish to experience real love, peace, happiness, health and abundance in our lives, we need to do all we can to create the sensation of this energy within ourselves to be able to attract this energy all around us.

Should there be any discord, disease, conflict or hostility in your life, you need to be completely honest with your-self and your role in its creation and be fully committed to your healing of any fearful, negative experiences you have created. Acknowledge any pain, wound, emotional instability, anger, resentment, grief, blame or engrained energy and make friends or allies with your discord to commence the healing, clearing process. Understand your involvement in the creation of your situation. Observe your continual feeding of your wounded stories' energy and use the power of your spirit to find another way for you to face and deal with this discord forever. Each experience, each drama, each tragedy, each wound re-creates us. You can be overcome and succumb to your drama or trauma to perpetuate your suffering or you can choose to rise and prevail stronger, more vulnerable and more invincible than ever. You may not accept this in a moment, although you will and you will emerge knowing the truth of who you are.

Love—I release everything that I am not.

LET GO OF RESISTANCE

It is our human nature to question and resist the possibility of change, particularly if they originate from the intuitive messages of the heart. We have long accepted that if we cannot think, believe, prove and rationalise opportunities that present, then they are not worth following because they do not exist in our reality. For the majority of us this has been the truth in most of our lives. However for the special ones who do not dance to the tune of commonly held beliefs and thinking, these intuitive creators live with the beat of their own hearts clearing away any doubts, obstacles and resistance that stand in the way of their dreams. Through time all the great masters, inventors, explorers, adventurers, inspirational sages and change leaders possessed these essential qualities and attributes to actualise their new instinctive vision for how life can be. It is their special attitude to life that sets them apart from the rest of us. They do not subscribe to consensus or group thinking, they dare to dream big, stand strong in their truth, constantly question and test the accepted normality, share their vision openly and live their dream in all of their life. Who they are is not defined by what they do. Their life philosophies are openly demonstrated by how they live and share their passion in every moment.

You too have the potential and capacity to be one of these inspirational people when you cease holding your-self back. The only limitation and restriction we have resides inside, not outside of us no matter what our life situation may be. It is accepted that some soul journeys may be more challenging than others although this just reflects the mighty power these souls have created for their evolution. Consider that we have all been everywhere, done everything and had everything done to us in every life we have lived. Have real compassion and empathy for others in their suffering for you have been where they may be. Ask your-self are you achieving all that you set your intention to achieve in this lifetime or have you given in or up, resigned or retired from really living. Are you still procrastinating or denying your truth and resisting the opportunity and possibility of re-creating and re-inventing your-self? After all, your life is still your responsibility and experience to live.

Let go of everything that is not the full potential and expression of the infinitely creative and loving being that you really are. Resistance or denial of needing to change amplifies and feeds the extent of the change that will be required. We cannot thrive in a comfortably numb and degenerative state. This is not living; this is just a mundane existence. Take charge of your life, treat each moment as precious, make new decisions often, question and test the reality of all things, accept nothing on face value, trust your feelings, listen to your intuitive senses, find your loving answers, live your life positively with love, honour and humility in all you do. You will find that by simply changing your beliefs and your perspective, you will not have to change all of your life. You will just change how you go about living life and everything around you will shift positively as a result of your new intention.

Love—I am free to be all of my-self.

CLEARING PATTERNS

You may not be aware that most of your life is sub-consciously driven by programs that have determined your vibration frequency in every lifetime. As you accumulate more negativity and fear, your vibration becomes darker and heavier thus limiting the potential of this life and every incarnation until you change your consciousness. No-one else can do this for you or magically heal your discord. Others may show you a way, but it is still your responsibility to create your change. When you decide to clear this patterning to be more positive and loving within your-self, you will be lighter in every way. It cannot be stated any simpler than this and you do know the difference between light and dark, just as you know night and day. Some of us find comfort in the familiarity and attention that our wounds, depression, drama and helplessness provide. Just because this sad, sorry energy has been with us for so long, it is not who we are and there is more to life than living in the self-imposed confinement of our own misery.

In each incarnation, your vibration, your state of being determines the quality of all your relationships and your evolution in each life. It is this vibration at your point of departure from each life that connects with the parents you have chosen for your next life. Think on this for a moment and you will realise the responsibility you have for your creation. Your family has done nothing to you nor are they to blame for your life being as it is. You decided to join them based on the vibration determined by your consciousness in your previous life and the energy and programs you intended to clear and heal in this lifetime. All energy is a continuum. You can only know what you know and you can only heal what you know.

Your patterns, conditioning and memories are influenced from the moment of conception to when you start taking conscious responsibility for your spirit's existence. How you are conceived, carried in the womb, treated and loved as a young child, triggers your soul's consciousness for this life's learning deep inside your sub-consciousness. This is then enhanced or retarded by your conscious programming and conditioning that takes place during your schooling through to your teenage years. During this stage of life, you may have started to question what you have been led to believe and start rebelling against established power structures and beliefs. In adulthood all of these programs come together beautifully and you may be shocked to find your-self subscribing to or rebelling against the life of your parents. Sound familiar. If we have not cleared all the patterns, conditioning, habits and rituals that we brought in with us and were rekindled by our families, we will continue to live life as we always have. Either way it will still be our patterns that are driving our beliefs and behaviours. It is still your responsibility to change and you can simply do this by knowing your-self, listening to what you know is right for you and decisively following your path.

Love—I am clear and walk my path lightly and lovingly.

SEVERING KARMIC LINKS

Karma is the word we associate with the transfer of energy through time and space. What you give out is what you will receive back, what you sow, you will reap or as you live, so too will your life be. It is unfortunate that we have interpreted karma as only a negative energy without considering the positive possibilities. Karma is far more powerful in the positive sense than it could ever be used negatively. Everything in existence is energetic. What you feel is interpreted, analysed and critiqued by the mind and how you think is how you will create and express your words and your actions will then reflect these thoughts and words. Your feelings, thought, words and actions release your energy, therefore creating your karma.

Your core feelings on any matter will always be positive, loving and honouring to you. As your feelings are engaged by your mind, your programming and beliefs take over the processing and the clarity of your thoughts will be determined by your consciousness and health of your mind. Should your thoughts be insecure, fearful or negative, this will be how you think, express and act, negatively influencing your experiences. To effect real change in your life, you need to be consciously aware of all your thoughts, how you feel and where you focus in each moment. This requires constant attention and effort on your part and also requires self discipline and responsibility for your creations. With practice, you will be more aware of the simplicity and clarity of each moment provided you are grounded and present.

There is a whole field of work focussed on speaking to the other side, clearing past lives, spiritual tourism and voyeurism and people wanting to know where they have been. As we are all essential elements of the universal body of all there is, we are connected to all experiences and energy through all existence. Presuppose that you have had thousands of lives, past, present and future. You have done everything and had everything done to you in every way that you can imagine and you will be close to visualising your infinite nature. We are all part of everything and as such, experience everything there is at some level. It has been my experience that each of us will be attracted to the energies that we need to amplify our souls memory sufficiently for us to access our truth. If you are drawn to a particular process, information or teachers, follow this guidance, you will find your way if you tune into what is right for you. All I know and have experienced is that if you deal with your life as it presents to you and clear your negativity and fears in each of these moments, you clear your energy through all time and space. Sometimes delving into or living in the past, just brings this energy into your current reality therefore increasing what you have to deal with each time. If this is what it takes, then this is what it will take.

Love—I let go of all my karma to be clear and free to live this life fully.

TAKE BACK YOUR POWER

Now is the time for you to take back your power from everyone and everything, including from your spirituality. Whenever you are outside of your-self or seeking your answers other than from within you, you are giving your power away to others. This is still denying that you have all your answers inside of you. This is not to say that others cannot guide or show you the way for only the foolish or arrogant ignore the wisdom and experience of others. Another can only illuminate your path; they cannot or will not be walking your journey for you. Only you will totally know all of your-self for only you have undertaken your soul's journey in your way through every lifetime, shaped and gifted through your energies experience. Just as a finely cut diamond is multi-faceted and crafted by the pressures of its creation, this too applies to your spirit. We are multi-dimensional, multi-faceted, unique diamonds of universal creation and as you evolve becoming more aware of your various aspects you will continually view different perspectives of your-self.

Whenever you are holding others responsible for your life, for how you feel and how things have turned out for you, you have given away your ability to change your circumstances. Look around you and you will find numerous examples of extremely courageous people who have dragged themselves through far more traumatic and horrific experiences to live fantastic, meaningful and worthwhile lives. The common denominator in all of these people is their inner strength and ability to rise above all that life has presented to them. Each of these souls would have received assistance, however it is still their responsibility to follow their guidance and do something with it. No-one has ever achieved anything by doing nothing. You will never have all of your answers in an instant, just follow your guidance in each step and your clarity will present as you are ready.

Review each aspect of your life and how you are living it and honestly look at where you give away your power whether it is through your beliefs, habits, family, work, behaviours, addictions, compulsions, obsessions, rituals, practices, games, health, energy, relationships, culture, country or spirituality. If any of these energies are restricting or limiting you, holding you from being the best you can be, then it is time for you to look at how you can take your power back, peace by peace. You will know that you are coming back to who you really are when you feel strong and at peace with where you find your-self. Peace is your soul's harmonic resonance with your environment and is your barometer that you are on track with your energy. When you feel removed from this harmony, you will know that you have been forgetful and strayed off your path. Throughout our lives we have oscillated between ecstatic highs and desperate lows in our vain attempts to find peace, balance and harmony. These energies are not found in these extremes. Resonance is in the balanced nothingness of the middle ground. Being able to deal with nothingness, where nothing is real nor matters is another challenge that you will face. With absolute nothingness you will create with pure and clear intentions.

Love—I take back my power and energy from all existence.

SELF BELIEF

When you have invested your time developing your understanding and knowledge of who you are, you will really believe in all of your-self. You will have grown through who you were not, made your errors in judgement and experienced your own knowing of life. You are not your role, sexuality, qualification, fame, what you create or do or even human. These manifestations are just your sensory vehicle to physically experience your spirit. The essence of who you are is pure energy, love, light and truth. Your spirit is the connection you need to know all of who you are and what you are about. Without this connection, you will only be scratching the surface of your full potential and existence. When you know and embrace your spirit, you will be all of your-self in all that you create and this is vastly different from just existing in a finite material world.

True belief in your-self requires no acknowledgement, approval or acceptance from anyone else other than your-self. No-one else will ever know all of you as you do your-self. I live for the day when everyone knows and accepts themselves fully to be able to really know and embrace others. Until this time of enlightenment, we can only accept and believe in others to the extent that we accept and believe in ourselves. This state of being is reflected in our highly critical, judgemental and intellectual world where everything that has not been proven scientifically bears no credence or acceptance in the wider community. Spirituality is an interesting concept for science where proven facts are constantly being reshaped and remodelled as greater information or different perspectives come to light. As a curious, inventive species we are constantly discovering new possibilities and understanding of how and why we are here. We all have a valid role to play based on our cosmic consciousness and it is important that we do all we can to play our roles well. We all have a place and ability to contribute to the greater good and prosperity of all souls incarnation.

Dare to be different and take your opportunity to create with loving intention to assist your-self and others. Listen to your spirit, formulate your own ideas, follow your guidance and create your life the way you desire it to be without imposing upon or negatively affecting anyone else. This is the truth of your soul's purpose and when you find what is right for you, you will clearly know your-self and what you need to create next. This truth will be enough to sustain your journey, clearing your way home to you and allowing your life to flourish beautifully and magnificently before you. Just listen to your intuition, follow your heart and know that you are enough for your soul's purpose. Believe in your-self to follow your dreams.

Love—I know and believe in all that I am.

SEE THE BEAUTY WITHIN

Embrace the true energetic nature of your spirit to feel all the beauty and power of who you really are. You are already stunningly beautiful and magnificent just as you are right now. If you are challenged in accepting this truth, just shut your eyes and bring your attention within your-self to engage the energy of your soul. Your essential energy is pure love, light and truth. Feel this energy come alive in every cell in your body, feel into your lighter self and you will know your true beauty. This process may take some practice to connect with your feelings. Just remember, all energetic flow starts with your core intention and ensuring your energy is clearly focused on your intended direction. You are a beautiful, all knowing energetic being of pure loving light and if you still have doubts, you have not quite accepted all of your-self yet. Trust your process for you will find you, I promise.

You are not your physical appearance although your body communicates how you are currently carrying your energy and where you need to focus. Your healthy spirit creates your healthy heart nurturing a healthy mind and healthy body. Any molecule of negativity or fear will reverse or contaminate this flow of positive energy. Negativity and fear pollute just like oil fouls water. This is the order of energetic flow within all of us. Your physical body is the vehicle of your spirit, it is your experience of this life and it suffers the blows and enjoys the sensations you create for it. Your body is very resilient, continually regenerating and renewing itself and is capable to enduring just about everything we put it through. When we are finished with this worn out vehicle, our soul simply leaves the body behind to find another means of evolution. Reincarnation is a beautiful and miraculous process enabling you to experience the joyful beauty of all souls, the earth and the universe.

The beauty of your soul will always shine through you even if you do not fully believe in your-self. We all have the spark of light within us patiently waiting for us to recognise and embrace our full soul potential. You are not who others think you are nor can you be compared to the shape or style of another. We are all unique individuals and share our energy differently in our own perfection. Acceptance of how you physically appear is a great starting point. Dealing with any of your undesirable aspects by taking full responsibility for taking action to change your-self is the next step. Then you must have the self respect and discipline to follow through in every part of your life. There are no half measures with spirit and there is no retreating from consciousness once you have set your intention to achieve real meaning and purpose in your life.

Just ask your-self one question, what am I prepared to do to create the life I desire? Then let this energy go to flow beautifully towards this purpose and ensure all your thoughts, words and actions fully support your intentions.

Love—I am a beautiful being of pure love, light and truth.

SELF LOVE

The essence of who you are is love, pure and simple. Have you felt this energy within you and do you know how to recognise or feel your own love? We often feel love from another, an animal or in the environment although can we identify our feeling of love in its simplest terms. Our human interpretation and manifestation of love has become distorted and manipulated to the point there is considerable confusion on what love really is. This too is okay for I have found that confusion always seems to precede enlightened clarity anyway. Throughout history there have been many heroic and mythical stories of great love brought to life in stories, plays and poems. Spirit's great story telling medium, the movie industry has been very effective in provoking our senses in regards to romantic love and all its variants. However is this really the love you have felt inside of you? From my experience we seem to dance around the subject of love with passion and romanticism without really surrendering to the vulnerability and freedom of real, deep and everlasting love that exists within all of us.

The definition of love that works best for me is one of absolute freedom. When I am free, unrestricted, unlimited, simple and positive, I feel and know my loving self. Whenever I feel controlled, obligated, conditional, negative or fearful, I know that I am not in a clear or loving space. When you really know your love for you, you will feel this love in every element of your being. You will know the pure energy of your-self and you will know real love. When you are seeking love from outside of you without first being this love your-self, you will always be searching to fulfil a need that is solely your own. To be open to receive love from another, you must attune your-self to the level of love you desire to create. The flow of all energy within or through you requires you to be the very energy you wish to feel. You must be the energy you wish to attract. You must give to your-self as you would like others to give to you. Otherwise you will have no sense or feeling of this energy. It is that simple, like attracts like.

With the pure freedom of love comes absolute responsibility for all your creations. Through knowing your-self, you will discover your love's energy and the real power of who you are. Your love is your connection to all the energy of the universe and through your love you will express the truth of your spirit in this physical form. It is therefore important that you fully comprehend the true nature of spiritual love, your connection to all existence and the role you have to play in actualising your love in human form. You are here to be love and to share your love. This is the purpose for your incarnation. Wherever you are and whatever you do, you are to be love.

Love—I am love in all that I am.

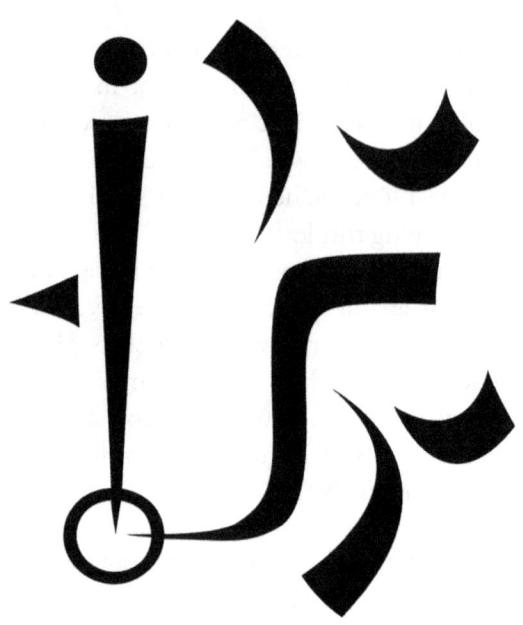

SELF WORTH

When you begin to know and accept all of who you are, you will know the true worth and value of your soul's energy. You are a beautiful and magnificent being of pure love, light and truth fully connected to all the knowing energy of the universe. Have you fully accepted this as your reality yet? You will know you have truly accepted your soul's energy when you are living its essence in all that you are. You will know the true power of your-self, the true worth of your soul and the real value of your life purpose. Having a true sense of self worth empowers and liberates you from the shackles of needing approval and conformity. Through your own experience of your own energetic creativity and soul knowing, you will know the true worth of your own uniqueness. There will be times when no-one else will understand or accept your point of view and that too is okay. You do not need to convince or convert anyone else to your beliefs and way of living. As long as you create experiences that shift your consciousness, you will have done what you were required to do. You are not here to please or rescue another soul.

You do not need acceptance, approval or validation of another to justify your soul's evolution. This journey is unique to you, revealing the loving truth of your soul's energy in its own way. Providing you accept and embrace your own uniqueness, in time others too may catch on. In knowing the true worth of your-self, you will know exactly what is right for you and you will know how to share your truth, softly, humbly and always with love. All that is important is you understand and know you are doing what you need to do for your-self and your way is not the only way or necessarily the right way for anyone else. Live your truth with love and compassion and through your example, you will show others their way.

Be who you were born to be. Share your love freely and responsibly with others and the universe. Live the truth of who you really are in all that you do and you will know your worth. In time, you're living and loving light will shine upon others. Each of us needs to feel for ourselves and discover there is more to life than what we have been taught to see and believe. Be the experience you wish to share and others will feel the worth and warmth of your soul touching their soul, therein lays your connection. It is the worth of your life that is important for you to value and live in every moment. You are as all spirit is and you know this to be true for you.

Love—I am worthy of all the greatness of the universe within me.

FAITH IN YOUR-SELF

Having complete faith in your-self and what you are about, is all the faith you will ever need. In moments of self doubt or forgetfulness, all you need to remember is your spiritual essence and go within your-self to find the answers to all you need to know. Faith is your ability to believe in all of your-self, particularly when you are testing or challenging your life. Faith is generally attributed to a belief in the unknown, mystical, esoteric, mythical or a greater external force that will make everything all right. My faith is an extension of the knowing belief and sensory connection I have with my-self, the planet and all existence. With this connection you do not need to blindly accept an energy or force greater than your own. You will know that you are within this greater body, a vital soul element implicitly connected within the whole universe. You are not separate or less than this body as you are created in the physical image of this energy.

Therefore, you do not require faith to believe in something that you are not personally familiar with. You will have complete faith in knowing who you are and knowing that you are spirit. This faith is not born of delusion or wishful thinking; it is developed through the experiences and results you have achieved by loving all of your-self. When you stand in your power, shining your light as only you can, you will stand strong and true, unswayed or undeterred by anything in your soul's way home. You are here to be true to your-self, with faith and strength, walking the light and love of your spirit. Remember who you are and you will know your truth.

You have always been this same person. The ideal representation of your-self has always been with you even when you choose to learn the hard and painful way. All of these hurtful, forgetful, destructive and fearful experiences have brought you right to this moment. You would not be who you are today if you had not created or experienced all your evolutionary events. Accept the perfection of this imperfection, the painful obstacles and opportunities you have created and acknowledge that you have found your way. Your inner faith and belief in what you are about has prevailed and prospered. You have remembered who you are and that is all that really matters. It is not important how we come to our spiritual realisation, it is just important that we do.

Love—I have complete faith in my spiritual purpose.

SELF VALUE

By living the loving truth of your soul's energy, you will always honour and serve the purpose of life. Every being in existence has universal purpose whether they are aware of its nature or not. Nothing is ever without reason or intention. Everything in existence has a meaningful role to play. When you have found your unique role, you will know exactly what you need to do and you will know the true value of your-self and your role. In our physical lives, our roles have traditionally determined the value of the energy exchange or income we receive for the work we do. When you step into your spirituality as your way of life, how you value your-self, not so much about what you do, will determine the real value of this exchange. We are all living in a physical existence where there is an accepted form of energy exchange that takes place for goods and services we require to sustain our physicality. This model is not perfect, sustainable or fairly distributed however until the day when we can all share equitably and lovingly, it is the model we have.

When you really value who you are and what you have to share, you will find that others will value you similarly. That is not to say that you overly value your-self or feel that you too need to chase the money gods. It just means that you will receive true value for what you share and create real value in your relationships on all levels. You will be open to receive an abundance of energy flow in all its forms and you will know how to share your prosperity for the greater good. I feel that when you have the ability to really create an abundant flow, this energy is not meant to accumulate or stagnate. Abundance is meant to flow freely for all to share. When you are in a position to assist others to find their soul's purpose, do all you can to help them find their way. This will enable your value to add real value to the lives of others and so on your energy will flow.

You do not take any of your possessions, wealth or relationships with you into your next incarnation. You will however take the consciousness of your vibration resulting from the soul work you have successfully undertaken in every lifetime. This is the true measure of the value of your worthwhile contribution to the conscious evolution of all spirit. You have soul purpose and through fulfilling your destiny, the real value of your evolution, your consciousness, your spirit will perpetuate long after you have completed your journey in this body. Value your role and your knowing. What you have to share is important and worthwhile; all you have to do is realise the truth of your love. Be your love, you will know.

Love—I value all of my-self, my gifts and all of life.

TRUST IN SELF

Trust is the basis of all relationships and if you do not have absolute trust in your-self and what you believe, then you will find it difficult to have trust in others. Just like all other energies that you desire to create in your life, you can only receive the energies that you have already given and experienced within your-self. Therefore it is essential that you must first trust your-self in order to trust others and for them to trust you. To trust without knowing is blind faith, not trust. To be able to trust anything to be true for you, you need to be able to know and accept the core of whatever it is you are trying to understand and this includes all of your-self. If you do not know who you are, you will not accept and trust your-self or anyone else for that matter.

For too long we have ignored the energy of our spirits in order to fit and prosper within the confines of this physical existence. It is true we are on this earth and need to sustain ourselves, however if this intention is divorced from your spirit, you will always feel incomplete. Otherwise you would still be out in the world, striving, acquiring, doing your next deal and whatever you think is required to be physically successful in this life. The very nature of you being here now, you are questioning and seeking greater meaning in your life. You may find some guidance and clarity in my words, however until you go within your-self to get to really know your-self, you will still be trying to physically think your way to your feeling of spiritual knowing.

Unfortunately too many of us have taken the hard, suffering and challenging path to understand ourselves and this has been the traditional, accepted way that we have been seeking spirituality for eons. Upon reflection you will know that if you keep doing things the same old way, you will continually re-create the same old outcomes. We often seek the answers in past and ancient practices and while these old belief systems and rituals are of use for you to remember a part of your-self, they will not be all of who you are right now. Who you are today is a unique combination of every experience, craft and gift you have acquired in every lifetime cumulating in the very special light being of pure love that you are today. I do not feel that we have reached this stage in our evolution previously. The vibration of ourselves and all existence has not been at this level in a long time. Therefore it is essential that we bring ourselves into alignment with this vibration by tuning into where we are right now, bringing forth the gifts and energy that is required to assist our transition to a much higher space of love consciousness. When you know you, you will trust you.

Love—I accept and trust all of my-self.

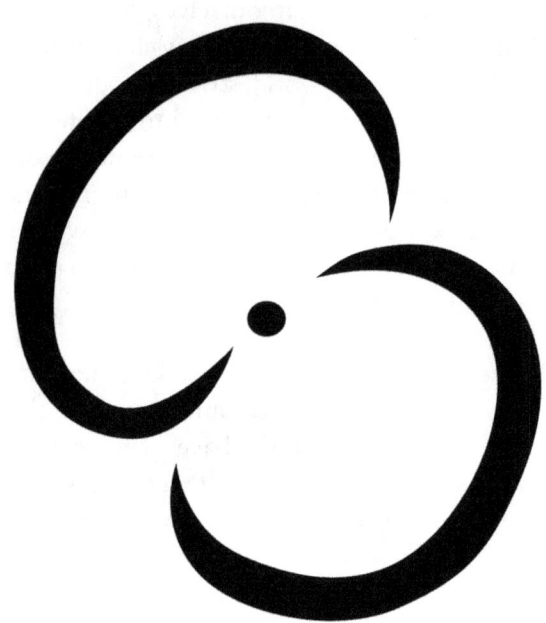

SELF CONFIDENCE

When you are able to really know, accept and trust all of your-self, you will experience complete faith and confidence in your-self. You will accept all of your own guidance, you will listen clearly to your inner voice of universal wisdom and you will innately know exactly how to initiate and respond in every moment of your creation. You already know you; all you need to accept is the full power of your own energy. All of us have all the universe within us, all you have to do is know this to be true for you and surrender to the flow of your energy. This potential, what you may admire in others is already within you. The fact that you observe and are seeking these qualities is an indication that you already recognise a greater reality and have set your intention towards knowing more about your spiritual life. Have confidence in your-self; walk faithfully and confidently on your path. Sometimes it pays to imagine your-self in your ideal stride in order to find your pace and your space.

The beauty of the spiritual journey is that we are all the same, we are all unique and we are all definitely special although no more special than another. While having some ego is essential for human growth, being egotistical and arrogant is not. Having confidence is not having a big head, standing at the pulpit or having millions of followers. Having confidence is having the ability to walk your truth, humbly and lovingly, assisting where you are invited and enabling other souls to stand strong in who they are. For those who are called to stand out to show the way, do not lose sight of who you are and how you came to your awakening, for you are still on the same journey and in the same body as everyone else. There is no power struggle in spirit, just enlightened consciousness.

Be confident and have complete faith in your awareness and unique perspective of life. While your view may be similar to the creation of another, it will not be the same, it will be uniquely yours crafted from your experiences and knowing of your life. All creative energy has the same source and when you are creating, you are coming from your spiritual core. When you create from your soul, it is your soul that you place on display for others to comment upon and this can be quite challenging if you have not dealt with your issues and insecurities. It is also true that if you intend to use your gifts as a business, this is perfect and to be encouraged. However be aware that you are not just dealing with business and money, you are nurturing and enabling your customer's souls. This is possibly the greatest responsibility you will ever undertake and should not be taken lightly.

Love—I am fully confident in my knowing and my ability to live my truth.

RELEASE YOUR POTENTIAL

Through your efforts to understand your-self, you will realise and release the infinite potential that exists inside of you. You will have tapped into your connection to all the energy the universe has to share. With awareness you can consciously channel this energy in every moment and as you conduct this energy through you, you will share your over-flowing energy with others. Draw this energy through you; be conscious of anything happening inside of you. Be fully aware of what your feelings are telling you and you will receive unique insights previously unknown to you. This gift is within all of us, accessible to all and available to everyone who chooses to remember who they are. This is the potential of all of us and this energy is meant to be shared. There has never been a greater need or more soul's incarnation than there are now.

Use all of the tools, guidance and insights you become aware of to understand all of life. Take in what works for you and let the rest be.

You will know what resonates with you, be aware of any self sabotage and use what you feel is right for you. Unlock and release all of your potential in whatever form that takes, whether it is creative, artistic, energetic, prophetic, physical, caring, nurturing, teaching and so on. Your unique gift will manifest for you to understand and heal you. When you find your love, you will know what you love doing. Create with real passion and understanding that all creation comes through us. Creativity is spirit's method of expressing itself through our hands. You will spend time playing creatively and freely, watching your hands move without conscious effort, just try to stay out of your way. It is true that if you do what you love, do what makes your heart sing, you will not work another day in your life. We are all here to contribute regardless of sex, age or environment and it is never too late to shift your consciousness.

It is never too late to fulfil your purpose. There are no valid reasons for you to ignore or deny the unique talent that is your spirit. You are gifted, your spirit's yearning has journeyed through infinity, acquiring and developing your energetic speciality. We really do not have any idea of how special and powerful each of us are. Look around you and there is abundant evidence of souls heeding their call, assisting, nurturing, caring, sharing, teaching, guiding and transforming their lives in their own way. Acknowledge your soul, embrace all of your-self and allow your energy to shift with your flow. You have infinite potential and capability to be all of your-self. Be honest with what is holding you back and release your-self to be all that you can be. Let go of your fears and doubts and allow your-self to be.

Love—I realise and release the full potential of all my gifts.

REMOVE ENERGETIC HOOKS

Wherever you go, wherever you are from, you will have acquired energetic attachments and hooks. These attachments do not serve or honour your spiritual journey, nor do they make your life any easier. Your energy field, your aura is far greater than you can imagine. Your aura is constantly filtering and feeling its way through your environment. If you can imagine your spirit fully in your body, your aura is a pure crystalline ball of light extending beyond your body for at least a metre in all directions. When you are with other people, particularly intimately, your auric fields move through one another and can even be completely immersed within each other. Physically we clean and release from our bodies on a regular basis, although how often do you clear other people's energy from your energetic body.

Every time we indulge ourselves in our own negativity, fears, projections, anger and judgement we are sending this energy out all around us and we are also open to have these same negative projections from others to attach themselves to our energy field. It does not take much to imagine or visualise how much energetic rubbish is floating all around and attaching to us. Have you ever wondered why after an argument, a big night out or visiting busy places that you come away feeling hung over or not quite your-self. This is not just created by the substances you consume, you absorb the prevailing energy around you that can pollute your state of being. When you start to listen to your feelings and begin clearing your energy field, you will become far more sensitive than you already may be. You cannot be vulnerable and not feel. Armouring or protecting your-self against negativity and fear also blocks your ability to feel love or truth. Your light is all the protection you need.

There are a number of intentions you can set to lessen the impact of this negativity. Firstly set your intention regularly to remove all energetic hooks and attachments. Clear your energy field of all energy that is not your own and does not serve you. Do not project any of your negativity or fears onto anyone else. As you clear your energy field, you will realise whenever you think, express or create negative intention toward another soul, you really only re-create this negativity within your body and it is you who will suffer your consequences. We all have sufficient fears of our own to face without projection or taking on the dramas created by others. As you remove your negativity and fears, you will feel lighter and more liberated than you have for many lifetimes. The clearer you become, the more sensitive you will be to your environment and greater knowing will form in your consciousness. Be aware of all the energy you take on and send out real love to create this love in your life.

Love—I remove all energetic hooks and attachments from my energy field.

CLEANSE YOUR AURA

You are a pure loving being living the truth of your light. Do you always feel the reality of this loving energy vibrating through all of your body? Are there times when you feel in the flow and other times when the flow is thick as soup? Commit to your memory the free feelings of your light body and develop some effective processes to help find your way back to your pure feelings. I regularly clean my auric field particularly when I am dealing with healing and channelling energies. When you open to your senses and start channelling energies, it is important to continually clear off energies that are not your own. I do this symbolically as well as energetically imagining all the light of the universe washing through me, dissipating and transmuting any energy that is not loving, serving or honouring my spiritual well being. I clean my spiritual body constantly throughout the day and more often than

I clean my physical body. Whenever you feel out of sorts, clear your energy.

People wonder why the energy of others has such a huge impact on them. Well consider for a moment that everything is creative and those souls who sub-consciously choose to create negatively or fearfully are powerful creators in the negative sense. They may not realise it yet, they would be far more powerful and effective if they choose positivity and love as their motivation. However this is not the case and whenever you find your-self in these situations, it is important that you do not feed their fear and negativity with more fearful, negative reactions of your own. This is where clearing your aura is effective in separating your-self from these negative and fearful circumstances. As you remove your own accumulated garbage, you remove your receptors to similar energies, lessening the impact others can have on you.

Many of our young people are very powerful with this generation being more aware, connected and intelligent than ever. However their energy is being distracted and misguided by inadequate leadership, unlimited access to technology and reliance on stupefying themselves to the realities of their world. This has been the case for the last half century where our role models are superficial and spiritually bereft leaving a void to be filled by less honourable beings. While this is all in its perfection, if we could all learn to look after our spirit, we would not be seeking to drug and numb our lives. You can only hear your soul when you are clear within you. When we shroud out our existence, our fears and negativity are amplified and in our face. We will not be able to clearly deal with our truth and therefore seek to mask out our true feelings even more. Continued abuse in any form blows massive holes in your aura letting out your rubbish to float around with everyone else's rubbish before returning inside you. You will then not only have your issues to deal with, but you have taken on others issues. Remember always that your spirit is clear.

Love—I constantly clear my aura to hear the clarity of my soul.

REMOVE PROTECTION

Over many lifetimes experiencing just about all the soul needs to learn for its evolution and enlightenment, we have accumulated considerable negative, fearful patterning and conditioning in our soul memory. We have all been hurt, wounded, destroyed, manipulated, used and betrayed and we have also done likewise to others. All souls have suffered and created suffering, this seems to be the way that we choose to learn or so the evidence all around us suggests. To enable our survival and protection, we have all built up considerable armour over many lifetimes. There is a wonderful parable about the Knight in Rusty Armour that explicitly describes a life existing in an armoured state. The moral of this story is that if you have applied protection over many lifetimes, you may be successful in blocking out the negative, fearful experiences you do not want. You will also have created the very negative energy to support your reasons for protection. This self fulfilling intention will also sabotage and harm your chances of creating the beautiful loving and positive experiences that you seek and desire.

In our busy modern life styles, activity burdened, technology driven, mass urbanised living and with habitual consumption bombarding your senses, over stimulating every moment, it is challenging for any soul to survive intact with some sense of self without the need for heavy protection. All around us are messages of gloom, doom and despair, hard luck stories and tales of enormous conflict and suffering. You do not have to go far to hear or see negativity and fear in full control of people's lives. How do you sustain a real sense of love and positive energy in this environment without being dragged down to this level?

As with all the paradox of spirituality, you have to do just the opposite. Remove all of your armour and protection for nothing can ever really happen to your spirit that you do not invite or ask for at some level. Let go of all the protection you have built over every lifetime, remove any energy from your-self that is not positive love and allow your-self to become totally sensitive and vulnerable. You have survived this far and you will never create an experience or lesson that you are not capable of learning from. You will not set your-self up to fail. It is not possible for you to fail when you are learning and growing even if it does not appear this way at the time. As you let go of the need for protection, you will also let go of the need for this protection in the first place. Fear attracts fear. Love attracts love. It is that simple. When you are faced with a negative situation, seek the loving response and let love do its beautiful work. Love disarms and soothes all conflict. Come back to your loving essence and observe your life change magnificently. Love is your answer.

Love—When I am love, I am always protected by my Light.

LIGHT PROTECTION

Stand confidently and completely in the love and light of who you really are and you will always be protected. Surround your-self with your love and light in all that you are and you will not attract the shadows of fear and negativity in your life. There is no darkness where there is bright light. You have cleared your fears, wounds and negative patterns to achieve your current realisations and awareness. Your past fears and experience can only impact on this present moment when you give these issues energy and attention. Your past is not useful in your present and nor should it influence your future creations, unless of course you let it.

To stand fearlessly and courageously in your light requires focus, discipline and above all consciousness of everything that is going on within you. It is not important what is happening around you and these energies are only reflecting your point of focus. Come back to your-self and how you feel in every situation and you will understand your role in the creation of all your experiences. Be responsible for all that you feel, think, say and do and you will take complete ownership over your life. When you own your feelings and how you express all of your-self, you will take back your power and begin creating the flow of new, loving and positive energies in your life experiences.

Be aware of your environment, where you place your-self and how you make your choices. Awareness is being conscious of every little thing, every nuance, your soul whispers and every message you receive. When you are conscious of your-self, you will know what inspires and what hinders your spiritual and physical growth. Shine your light on all of your-self to become aware of all of you. Illuminate everything around you to determine the truth of your life. It is easy to turn on your own light, all you have to really do is flick the switch of your intention to understand and accept all of your-self (both the light and dark). For too long we have operated out of who we are not, through our fears, negativity, wounds, pain and our disconnection with spirit. It just requires your choice to change your life. Others cannot make your decisions nor can they do it for you. Only you can turn on your light and only you can secure your journey, making it safe for you to be all of your-self.

Love—I stand lovingly and courageously in the Light of my Spirit.

SEAL YOUR AURA

Your entire energy body is contained within your aura which surrounds your physical body. Your aura is your true spiritual body that energises and enables your physical body to experience all of who you are. It is through your aura that you feel; it senses everything, feels everything and is connected to the greater body of all there is. When you generate your energy, this energy runs through your body, through the planet and right throughout the universe. It is important that when you share this vital energy of life, that you share this energy through you and not from you. This is a subtle difference, however when you really understand that you are of the universe, that this universal energy is freely and infinitely available for all of us to share. Your physical body is very limited as an energy source within itself and as such can only provide the physical energy and experience contained within it.

Therefore your physical body acts as a conduit, a vessel for you to share your universal energy with your-self and others you connect with. To channel your energy, you need to be aware of your universal connection and how your energy uniquely manifests within your body. When you have spent time invoking your energy, feel how this energy channels through your body and you will know how you are to share your-self. As you generate this energy, you will illuminate all of your-self and you will understand your own gifts. All energy flowing through you should prompt your consciousness as it passes through you to others. Every being you attract to your energy field will represent life to you, broadening your perspective and provide special insights. Our respective energy fields amplify one another, each of us powerful and meaningful in our own right and here to assist each other's spiritual journey. In accepting this truth, you will know that nothing is wasted or lost, everything has intent and purpose. It is the conscious wise souls who will understand and utilise this energy to inspire and motivate our evolution.

We are all souls (cells) of energy in the greater body of all existence, with a vested interest in helping ourselves help others find our way home to our spiritual essence. As you are, your world will be.

Love—I share my energy freely and wholly with my-self and all others.

STAND TALL IN YOUR POWER

When you fully understand and accept your spiritual energy, you will take back your power from everyone and everything, including your spirituality. You are a unique and powerful soul of pure creation and when you stand strong and tall in your power, you will just know what and how you need to be. This knowing energy will emanate from deep within your soul's memory of universal creation. You are creating in every moment of life with every decision and act you create. Everything and everyone is creative whether you are aware or not. Most of us fear the real power of who we are and are reluctant to be exposed to the scrutiny and power of others. We have spent many lifetimes being less than who we are to fit in with others, to belong to tribal belief systems and to ensure that we are not persecuted or judged by our peers. Being powerful is not about your egotistical insecurities or the physical power of your position in society. Your spiritual power is about how you feel and how you positively contribute towards the evolution of your-self and all life. This is the real everlasting power of positive love.

Our experience with power structures and game playing has been influenced by how the energy of power has been used through the ages. Since our inception on this planet, there have been many examples of how we have misused and abused power. Many powerful souls have incarnated to teach us more about who we are not through their endless conquests, conflict, persecution, acquisition, empire, fanaticism and self righteous fervour. The lessons of history have taught us well as we continue to utilise these same fear inspired processes to combat conflict of our own creation. Rarely do we seek to resolve the actual cause at the heart of the problem. We all have vested interests lusting after our slice of the pie. Continually competing, fighting and harming each other to pursue our delusion of success. It seems most physical success has its motivational seed in personal insecurity and inadequacy. Dysfunction on some level appears to be a primary motivator for most achievement. This has been the energy that has inspired and driven humanity since our beginning.

Personal and collective success is highly commended, encouraged and available for all of us. However it is essential that the seed of this success is grounded by the awareness of its connection to whole body. When you understand your spiritual inter-connectedness with all life, your senses and decision making processes will become more considerate of sharing and benefiting everyone, not just your-self. You are not separate, we are not separate and we are all on this planet, in this universe together. When we play our respective roles lovingly and positively for the benefit of the whole body, we will then understand the real use of our spiritually inspired power. Your spirit has the real power, the absolute knowing connection with all energy and it is only your spirit that lives on further proving its power.

Love—I am the power of my own creation.

SELF RELIANCE

Being self reliant and independent may appear at odds with spirituality connectedness, however independence provides the central focus of your own path. We are all part of the tapestry of all life. Each of us is a unique thread of energy weaving our way with other inter-connected energetic threads. Together we all make up this beautiful and magnificent fabric of life. When you are walking your life your way in your truth, you are fulfilling this purpose. While we are one, we are not the same. Just as we are of many shapes, colours and creeds, we too are unique of spirit, shaped individually by all our experiences. Your spirit is just as independent as your body is. When you concede or subscribe to the views of others, you will give away some of your-self until you have few views of your own or any idea of who you really are anymore.

In coming back to your-self, listening to your soul's calling, you will realise how much of your-self that you have given away in your quest to belong to the illusion of life around you. You will realise that very few souls feel like they fit or have any idea who they really are and they may be the ones showing the way. In the search for your truth, seek out souls who are inspirational and freely sharing their positive message of love and infinite possibilities for peace and happiness. It will be these wise souls living their truth who have the best interests of the entire planet, human, plant and animal at the heart of all they are about. When you have connected with this energy within you, then strive to live your love, setting your example, your way. This is true independence as you are now utilising your love of all life to find your way to share with others.

It is okay to be different and unique. You do not need to fit with others point of view and you do not need to have others subscribe to your way of life either. As long as you respect that we are all unique, everyone is entitled to their perspective and everyone has the right to live happily, peacefully and freely in their own way. Being independent and self-reliant is not about being separate or isolating your-self from the world. You will be truly independent when you can stand lovingly in your truth regardless of where you are. Just be the best you can be in every situation you create and you will work it out. Trust in your-self and what you know. You know your way. All you ever have to do is love all of you.

Love—I experience my life through my spiritual body.

DETACHMENT

Detachment is freedom just as love is free. When you are no longer attached to this body, your spirit, physicality, other beings or things, including your belief systems and your emotional baggage, you will be free to be who you really are. You are meant to be a free loving powerful spirit of the universe. Everything in this life lives and dies, it is here temporarily, it has its purpose and then passes or shifts to its next existence. This is a fact and there has been substantial evidence in your life to support this truth. Everything and everyone has its time. Be sure to use your opportunities and gifts wisely with focussed intention.

When you observe life, you will see that we hold onto each other for the fear of being alone, unloved or unwanted, we kill ourselves working with little joy, honour or fulfilment just to make a living, we accumulate possessions that we soon tire of and cannot take with us, we think we have the answers even when they harm us and the planet, we hold onto traditions, addictions and beliefs that focus on negativity and fear, conflict and pain. There is an infinite list of the abnormalities and dysfunction in our lives, but does it need to be this way. Consider if you could just let go of one element of your life, what would it be and how easy would it be to detach your energy? It starts with a choice. Decide whether a particular issue, thing or person serve and honour your soul or not. It is this simple. All you have to do is change your choices to let it go forever. Everything we are attached to holds us fixed to that energy and restricts the flow of that energy in that space. Ultimately when you decide to leave your current body, you will leave everything behind, including your belief systems. You will only be taking your soul's energetic vibration with you, so at some time it is worthwhile to give this energy some attention.

Detachment is not about having nothing or no-one in your life. Being detached enables you to be surrounded by all of life without being attached to any of it. While this may sound fanciful, if not impossible, just give it a try. Select something that you thought you could not go without to survive, then let this thought, belief, habit, thing or even person go for a period of time and observe your reactions or responses. You will be surprised at how well you cope with your new freedom and you may even find that you receive more of a particular energy once you set it free to come back to you. Our attachments, grasping and holding onto stuff holds us fixed in a point in time. As you create your intentions, set them free to manifest without your interference. Liberated energy enables spiritual manifestation.

Love—I am free.

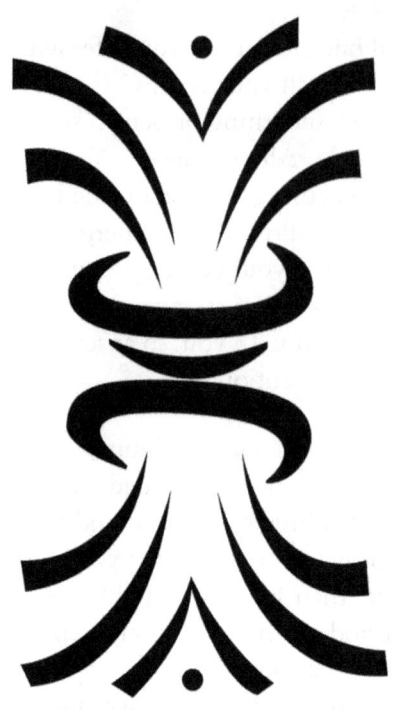

SOUL EXPRESSION

One of the most powerful forms of sharing the pure energy of your spirit is through the open expression of your soul's truth. You have the unique message and energy of your soul to share and through your connection to your essence, you will know how best to share all of your-self. Let go of all reservations, self imposed limitations, fear of judgement or the reactions of others. You do know who you are and you know your own energy. No-one can know you better than you know your-self and only you can express your-self in your own way. Allow your-self to be free to express all of your-self even if at the start you may be a little silly or radically different from others. It is just important that you express in whatever form it presents to you. Your expression of your energy will release and actualise this energy, making it real for you. As you allow your-self to express from your heart centre, you will share your love with the world. The love seed within your heart will be released to physically germinate. The full and honest expression of your love liberates this energy to actually manifest in your life.

Connect your heart and throat chakras to allow the full and open expression of your loving essence. If you have not learnt nor been encouraged to express your feelings verbally, try practicing with trusted friends who can show you how. In the beginning you may be a little clumsy or even unintentionally offensive, it is just important that you allow your-self to open up and speak up for you have a voice worth hearing. Undertake new creative pursuits that interest and challenge you. Try an art or craft that you have not had the confidence to attempt previously. Allow your-self to dance freely and sing loudly in public. Play an outdoor physical sport or game. Spend time in the natural world as pristine ancient country is a great teacher and healer (Nature feels and knows it all). Explore and express your sexuality to feel your connection with the divine, a true gift of being physically human. When you free your-self to fully express your spirit through your creativity, you will really connect with the creative source that is you. Your creative expression is your soul's expression of the universe, purely creative and free.

You are free to express all of your-self and what you have to say or share is important and it is essential that you materialise your knowing gift. The seed of expression within you is bursting to come into bloom. Through your inspiration, your play and experimentation, you will be given or awaken all the tools you need to release your light. There is nothing in your way that can inhibit, restrict or persecute you for being your love. You do have the ability and the power to fully express and be all of your-self. Let go of any excuses, patterns or doubts and let your love be free to be all that it desires to be. Express with love to create love in your life. Love enables, shares, nurtures and liberates your soul to be all you are meant to be. Your expression of your love creates this love in all your experience. Be your own creation of love, light and truth.

Love—I express all of who I am with love and responsibility.

OWNERSHIP AND RESPONSIBILITY

When you take ownership and responsibility for everything you have experienced in your creation of this life, you will have the power and ability to change your life. Self responsibility empowers and liberates you. Victimhood and blame just holds you in the misery and pain of your past. These negative energies disable your ability to make positive changes as you are still holding others responsible for what they have or have not done for you. While you are still blaming or judging others, you disempower and harm your-self. None of us has the ability to influence or change another. We all have the free will to make new choices, to make fresh decisions in every moment and when you start to take total responsibility for your-self and your life, you will set yourself free.

This is a challenging concept for most humans to accept as we have continually given our power away to our teachers, families, rulers, leaders, bosses, cultures, ideology, traditions, science, intellects, emotions, desires, wounds and addictions. We constantly place responsibility on others. We have an expectation that others know better and more than ourselves. The laws and structures of our civilisations also disempower us as they discourage individuality and creativity through regulation, conformity and compliance with the group order. Just have a look at the litigation and insurance systems; they are the most classic illustration of the projection of responsibility away from the individual. When we are able to consciously frame our way of living around the fundamental principle of self responsibility, we will start to see more responsibility undertaken by everyone for their own poorly considered choices. Everyone creates or plays a significant role in the creation of their experiences and as such must take responsibility for their role.

There are many times in recent history where we may have made different choices if we had taken a moment to consider the root causes of the conflict, had empathy and compassion for the other side of the argument and desired a more loving and peaceful resolution that benefited everyone. I have never understood violent conflict and continual negativity to be an effective solution to anything. That is not to say that this last resort option is sometimes necessary, however it should never be the first reaction. Violence, fear and negativity can only ever promote and foster more fear and negativity, regardless of the situation. We are better than this and we know better. Take full responsibility for your-self, for your feelings, thoughts, words and actions and you will experience the full power of who you really are. Always seek the loving, positive answers from within you and sometimes it is useful to create the space you need to find your love.

Love—I am responsible and own my creations.

SPIRITUAL FOCUS AND DISCIPLINE

Life will always be in balance, even when we are not. Your energy field consists of many sensory mechanisms, atoms, molecules, cells all vibrating at a frequency that creates your physical body and experience of life. When you consider your-self just to be your body and your role, you are denying the majority of your existence. For you are far more than your physicality. Your body is your vehicle of spiritual experience. It is the means for you to explore and discover all the possibilities for living your love through this physical life. If this has not been your experience so far, it soon will be.

The key energies that create your experience reside in your intellectual program's influence over your intuitively feeling heart. We have all been conditioned and taught to believe that all the answers we need can be acquired from external physical means through experience, education, work and the school of hard knocks. All I can offer here is that we have all done this to death with little solace over many lifetimes. If you still think your answers lie in your physicality, you are right to be on this path until you are not. If you feel like you are continually just going around in circles, different day same patterns, then just maybe you need to make some new choices.

Our science has shown that we only utilise a small portion of our brains consciously and we do not often connect with the larger brain I call my intuition or super conscience. The super conscience is connected to all existence and as such is connected to the infinite knowing of the universe. When you really access and integrate with your spiritual body, you will know this to be true for your-self. I have found that you cannot think your way to your spirit, no more than you can think your way to your feelings for these key energies are one and the same. To know your spirit, you need to know your feelings. To know your feelings, you need to unravel your negative emotional programming and your busy intellect in order to really feel. Letting go of the mind's power over you is an individual process requiring time, energy and discipline on your part.

Spend real time with your feelings to understand the difference between what you feel and what you have been conditioned to believe. Allow your-self to imagine and dream your new story of pure creation into being and you will begin to know your-self. When you access your soul truth, engage the power of your mind to sort pearls of wisdom you can utilise in your life, the insights worth knowing and observe then let go of anything that does not enhance and amplify your spiritual journey. You will know your balance point, your place of peace and harmony from where you can create your life from this clear, loving space.

Love—I am balanced of mind and spirit.

PEACE, BALANCE & HARMONY

Now you have arrived at the state of the serene heart you have desired and sought out for many lifetimes, how do you feel? We have all been searching for balanced equilibrium for as long as we can remember. When you experience this state of being, be with it and allow your spirit and body adjust to absolute purity of this balanced energy for it will be nothing like you have ever experienced. This was my experience of real balance for I was quite disturbed by the void of nothingness that I had created. We are all seeking greater peace, balance and harmony in our lives without considering what this really means in our reality. You can only know this place when you are really there. Balance is stillness, quietness in the mind and at peace in all of your being where nothing or nobody really matters.

Our expectations of life are often driven by external material achievements inspired by our fears, insecurities, dysfunction, wounds or any negative experiences from our collective pasts. We think that when we have all that we physically need, we will have the freedom to be who we want to be. Well if you have accumulated lots of possessions, aspired to the top of the corporate or professional tree, networked well and have your spirituality together, then congratulate your-self for you are truly special. If you are like the rest of us mere mortals, you may have struggled with or been suffocated by your acquisitions or achievements only to find the view wasn't anymore glorious the higher you climbed. If you have a feeling that something is missing in your life, you will be right and it will be in the last place you think. When we do not connect with our spirit, we will always be challenged with really connecting with anyone or anything else.

Through getting to know your spirit, you will strip away all the falsehood and illusion of your life, coming back to the simple, pure, beauty and love of your soul. When you are no longer seeking your answers outside of your-self or in your physicality, you will experience real peace, balance and harmony. You may find that nothing in your previous reality has the same meaning or even find that nothing or no-one feels real to you. Balanced nothingness can be challenging, however be with it, do not make radical or dramatic changes just yet, strive to sustain this feeling and let it integrate within all of your being. It is in this void that you will be able to create from a space of purity and clarity for you are no longer being driven by your sub-conscious fears, insecurities and inadequacies. Come back to the truth of your own love, find your loving answers and inspiration and live this love in all that you are and you will create your own miracles. Being at peace, balanced and in harmony with your world is your indication that you have done your inner work. You have arrived at your core, ready and able to actualise your spirit. Allow your-self to enjoy and have fun along your way.

Love—I am at peace, balanced and in harmony in all ways.

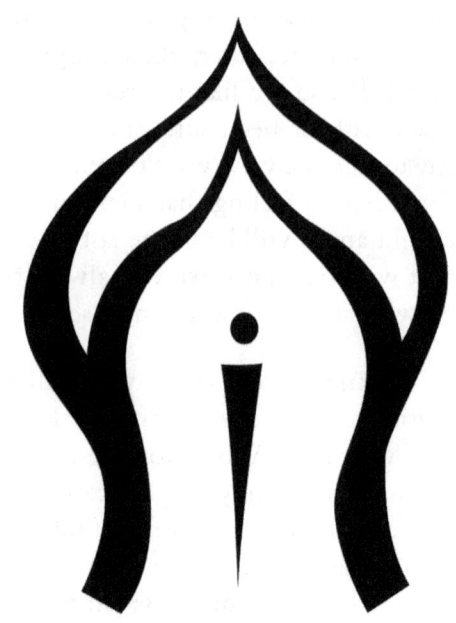

GRACE AND HARMONY

Live in the flow of your heart's energetic desire and you will feel the grace and harmony of your soul's destiny. Being in the energy of peace and balance enables you to connect with your own rhythm and vibration with life. Step outside your own truth and you will be buffeted back onto your path very swiftly. As you become clearer in your consciousness, any deviation from who you are will reflect quite obviously and immediately. Living with grace requires acceptance of the perfection of all things and harmony is the peaceful resonance you will feel when you are in grace. You will float effortlessly from one flower of life to another, amazed at the ease of your efforts and with pure gratitude for the universal energy that is you.

It is through this easy flow of energetic creation that you express and experience all of your-self. Consider that you are a powerful, loving being of pure creation accessing all the energy of the universe to manifest your spirit in this incarnation and you will be close to knowing your purpose. Accept your guidance, know your-self and trust that you know your way and your life will present beautifully before you. Only one piece of your puzzle will be provided in each moment and will require you to accept and act with real trust before you receive your next answer. Imagine your-self to be traversing a bottomless ravine to the other side of your-self. To cross-over to who you really are, you will need to take one step at a time, not trying to race ahead of your flow, trusting each step will be perfectly supported and you will feel your way. Any doubt, second guessing, procrastination, sabotage, fear or negativity will take you right back to your old self for you to begin your journey again. Be in your flow, trust your-self and allow your spirit to guide you.

You will know the peace and serenity of your own grace. You will be in complete harmony with your life and your creative intention will manifest beautifully and quickly before your eyes. It is important that you are focussed and aware of where you set your intention for these are the seeds of your own creation. Use your power lovingly and responsibly to create and share the pure energy of spirit that you are. You are not separate nor are you alone in your creation. The basic notion of your spiritual grace and harmony is your contribution to the greater good of all. Be loving, at peace and in grace with all life and this will be your experience of life.

Love—I am living and loving with grace and harmony.

GRATITUDE

With sincere gratitude and thanks for all of your life every day, you will release your power to create magnificently in all that you are. Gratitude is a powerful energetic creator for it will project the positivity of your energy forward to prepare your way for you. Being truly grateful is like the lubricator of all creativity in the positive sense. When we lack or neglect this very special energy or attribute, we sabotage and block everything we wish to create in our lives. We render ourselves powerlessness through being victims, undeserving, negative or fearful. If you think this will be so, then this will be your creation, therefore your truth. Until you really know that you are the creator of all your life experiences, you will always be challenged in acknowledging gratitude for your own creation. That someone you have been blaming can only ever be your-self. You found your way into this life and it is up to you to find your way through your life.

This is also true of the nature of "the universe will provide" or externalising your gratitude toward any external force. You are the source, power and instigator of your own creation and when you accept this to be your truth; you will truly accept your power to create anew. This is not to say that you should not be grateful for others or to unseen influences. Gratitude in all its beautiful liberating forms is essential. All I suggest is that you always acknowledge the part you have played in manifesting your own creative experience. You have created yourself in the image of and connected to all creation, therefore you are at the centre of your own experience. You are the hub around which all of your life revolves and evolves in your reality. The universe exists through your physical experience of your spirit. Your acknowledgement of gratitude within you and for you expresses this bountiful energy through all existence. Deny your own role in your creation and you will deny your creative essence.

Connect with your true self. Open your eyes and heart to the magic that is all around you. See the beauty within and surrounding you. Feel the energy of your soul and the energy of others. Share all of your love through your-self with those you meet. Walk softly and humbly, embracing your infinite love as your reason for being. Be grateful for everything you have realised and enacted in this life. Thank those souls who taught you who you were not, accelerating your journey to this point. Have real gratitude for your-self and the perfection of everything you have created thus far and be grateful of your powerful ability to create your life in every moment. Everyone that has played a role in your life has shaped, influenced, taught, guided you and shared your soul's experience. We are all connected, all one, hopefully learning and evolving into the beautiful loving soul's we are meant to be. Be grateful and appreciate every experience of your life and you will release your energy to focus on your present creation of life. You deserve to live and love a great life.

Love—Gratitude, attitude and passion inspire my evolution.

EMBRACE YOUR LIFE

Our Earth is magnificent, bountiful and beautiful, stunningly organised to sustain itself and all of us. This planet is our wonderful home, our garden and our paradise. We all live and love within her. Why is it then that we seem to do all we can to harm this magnificence? Many civilisations and generations have come and gone, all leaving behind somewhat less than they found. We use all the earth has to offer without ever giving much thought to how we can return the favour. Even the environmentally aware among us seem to come from a fearful, violent space which can only contribute to more destruction and desolation. Each of us needs to take some responsibility here to do all we can individually do to ensure that our own actions are doing no harm to ourselves, the planet or any other living being, plant or animal. This is not the role for particular souls, it is the role of every one of us and that means you.

Just as every cell, atom and molecule knows what is going on within your body in every moment, every soul, all energy in the body of this planet is connected and influenced by the health of the planet. Your soul's evolution is totally dependent on the evolution of the planet, intrinsically linked and immeasurably intertwined. There is no separation between you, the planet and all existence. Everything is completely involved within one another. We are all one. When you really accept this truth, you will feel everything there is to feel and you will know your role and place. If there is something missing in your life, then this is it. Just connect with life on this planet and you will begin to know you again.

It is that simple. We live with such abundance and beauty all around us with amazing potential for everyone to prosper, yet we still have souls experiencing extreme poverty, starvation, abuse, violence and exploitation all around the world. I do not understand the need for this imbalance even though I accept each soul's journey is self created. However I do believe that as we grow in consciousness, aware of the interdependence of all souls, that we will do all we can to enable and show each other how to be more loving, positive, compassionate, considerate, sharing and peaceful. We all have our role to play in this action and it starts within each of us. When we have these qualities enshrined in our way of being, this is the energy we will share with our loved ones and all those around us. You can only ever share the energy and intention that you have experienced within your-self. You must be the change you wish to experience in your world. Being your spirit is a full time role, it is not something you turn on and off as you please. Walking the truth and light of your spirit requires your full commitment and discipline to be who you are all the time.

Love—I walk my life in love and truth.

EMBRACE YOUR GIFTS

You are a very unique and special being of pure light, love and truth who has endured many challenges to manifest the beautiful consciousness of your being. Through the process of experiencing life in all its forms, you have developed many individual gifts and talents to help you understand more of who you really are. These memories have been crafted through many lifetimes and have formed the nature of your soul's energy. How you are and how you express all of your-self is unique to you. You are like no other; you are an individual energy, multi-faceted, shaped by your journey, polished through your work on your-self and created through your innate desire to be the best you can be. Just as our bodies are an individual reflection of how we carry our soul energy, our spirit is this same reflection of every experience we have been through. The energy that you bring forth into each life is the energy you intend to heal and clear with the gifts and abilities you have learnt along the way. This is your evolution.

As you journey within your-self, you will access these gifts even if you are uncertain or have no comparable basis in your previous reality. If you can imagine that you can create a particular energy, let your imagination be free to explore this infinite possibility. Allow your-self to dream and aspire without imposing conditions or limitations. Experience real changes in the quality of your life, accept your unique differences and have confidence to explore life in your own way. Our energy field will always create its own perspective and reality. This is our intended purpose. You are a free, loving and creative soul with your unique role to play. All you need to ask your-self is are you living the majesty of your uniqueness or are you still doing what is expected of you?

You know the truth of this question and know that it is time for you to set your-self free to be the love that is your-self. Freedom is love. You will know what is right for you. You will acknowledge all of the skills and qualities you have ever developed and you will know how you would like to live out this life. You will know and embrace the special gift of who you really are and you will know how you need to contribute towards the evolution of your-self, the planet and the universe. When you remember all of who you are, you will remember why you are here. Embrace all of your-self and create the life you deserve and desire. Believe in your own knowing energy to experience the real power of your own love.

Love—I embrace the powerful gift of who I am.

WALK YOUR PATH

You have travelled through many lifetimes experiencing all there is to experience in your own way. The accumulated energy of every one of these lifetimes has propelled you to your current reality. It is this energy that has sustained your lives, in each of them you have walked through your truth, evolving into the beautiful being of pure love that you are. It is not necessary for you to know exactly what you have come through to reach this point in your consciousness. It is just important that you are here right now. Accept that you have done all there is to do and you have probably had most things done to you. Sometimes our curiosity to know our past just draws the wounds or dramas of the past into your present life. Explore your past if this is necessary for your journey, although be conscious of bringing these issues into your reality. I have found that when you deal with your issues as they present in your current life, you will be able to deal with all these issues through time and space, the past and future. You have enough to face right now without needing to continually seek your truth in the false mirror of the past.

Bring your attention and energy into this current moment for this is the only space in which the truth really can exist. The past will always be distorted by perspective and the future is still yours to consciously create. Be aware of all of your-self, your feelings and your intentions in this moment. Establish honourable and loving intentions and actions. Focus on your dream life and take one trustful step at a time along your path to this life. With practice, you will clearly feel and see how you desire to live and love. This intention will set your journey on track which will evolve along the way as your awareness and clarity of purpose expands. You are ever evolving; you are not static nor are you the same in any two moments. You and the world around you are always changing, growing, renewing and shifting. When you are focused and centred in your purpose, you will flow and bend easily with the movement that is always around you.

Be flexible and open in your attitude and approach to life. Strive to be true to your core energy, to always honour your path and have the courage to follow your dreams regardless of the obstacles you create to test the strength of your character. Know and trust the love you have found within you. Live this love in all your actions and share this love freely on your path and this energy will flow back to you in great abundance. Only you can live your life your way for it is only you who knows all of you and knows what is really right for you. Stay out of your own way, release anything that is holding you back, trust that you know the way and let go in order to flow beautifully towards your destiny. Have the conviction and courage to let your-self flow with your energetic intention. You will love and enjoy the ride.

Love—I walk my path my way in truth and love.

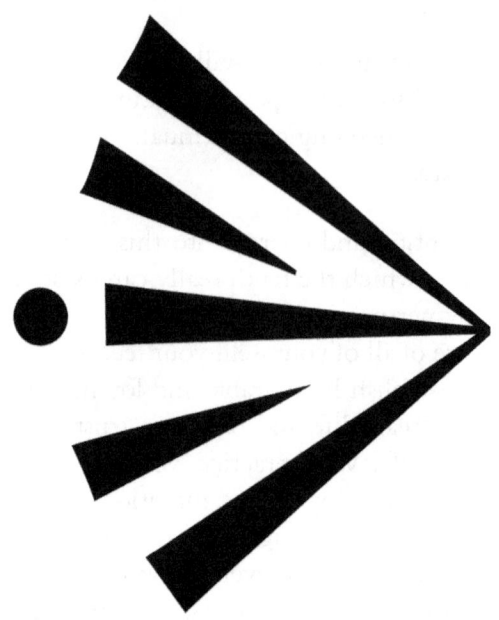

REPEL NEGATIVE, FEARFUL ENERGY

Whenever you turn on a light you are bound to attract the occasional moth. So too will the light of your love draw dark energies to you that will test the resolve of your spirit. It will take more than a sprinkle of fairy dust or the odd healing to clear away the accumulated fears and negativity we have drawn into our energy fields over many lifetimes. We seem intent on continually learning and suffering through negative or fearful experiences, intent in clearing our souls through hardship and pain. We are locked into the paradigm that if something is not hard work, complex or painful, then it isn't worth doing. I apologise for debunking this age old myth, however your path to your spirit should not be hard, painful or dramatic. If spirit is pure love, light and truth, why do we make our journey so difficult and painful?

Maybe we have subscribed to a common belief that has transcended time where the mystics, religious elders, shaman and enlightened ones of the past have done it the hard way and therefore it should be hard for us. Pause for a moment and consider the times in which they lived and what was necessary for this planet's vibration at that time. Now transport your-self to feel our current vibration and observe all the resources and information you have available to you. The ancients did what they needed to do in their time to prepare and show the way for us. You have incarnated in a different time and space with so much information and knowledge available to you, yet we seem to question more than ever. Once it was accepted that we were connected to each other and all existence. Now we are individualistic, self centred, greedy and consume at all costs, disconnected, without purpose or intent, living empty, materialistic lives devoid of real love and truth. Astoundingly now, we wonder what is missing and wherein lies the meaning or purpose.

You have never been at this stage in your incarnation in any lifetime and therefore the tools that were used in the past may not be as useful as they once were. I have found that many of the old teachings while relevant in their time may not have the same energetic impact in the current vibration. It is important that you rediscover the truth of who you are and the unique combination of gifts you have developed to assist the greater evolution of all existence. As with all evolving matter, we need to redefine and redesign what we are doing to find new and creative ways of carrying our energy lovingly into our collective future. Connect with the real power that is you, let go of any energies that do not serve or honour your path to start living the love of your life in all that you are. It is essential that you do all you can to share your love and light with your-self and all those around you. In creating this energetic and loving reality, you will be doing what you came here to do.

Love—I repel all energies that do not serve and honour my journey.

ATTRACT LOVING, POSITIVE ENERGY

All energy is creative and is drawn from the core of the universe. You exist within this greater body of all existence and as such, your energy is this same creative source. As you become aware of who you are, you will know how you create this reality you call life and how you influence the flow of energy all around you. For too long, we have ignored this creative ability, preferring to think that life just happens to us and that we are just pawns in a much bigger game. Well it is time to rethink this belief. You are the creator of your reality in both the positive and negative sense. If you have considerable negative experiences, very fearful or traumatised, phobic or even just not happy, this is an illustration of your ability to create negatively. Believe it or not, but the only common denominator in your life experiences is your-self. If you are continually repeating the same experiences in different circumstances, you are still the primary source of this creation and just maybe, you are the one that needs to change, not everyone else.

We prefer to believe that if only the world and everyone in it was lovingly perfect, then we would be at peace and happy. This is highly possible for the rest of the planet, however if you decide not to change with this changing world, you will still be where you are today. Just as you have powerfully created your negative experiences, you have even more power to create positively and lovingly when you really connect with the energy of your spirit. Everything in creation is in the flow responding to the frequency of the consciousness that it is connected to. To be involved in this flow, we need to shift our personal vibration to the level of consciousness that we wish to experience. You can only attract energies that your vibration connects with. Just as you have created negatively drawing negativity to you, try the alternative energy of positive love and observe how quickly your experience of life changes. This process requires awareness and focus. With practice, trial and error, you will see the differences that you can make in all aspects of your life. Take your time, select the easy targets first, allow your-self to succeed, then test your resolve and take on anything that may be sabotaging your own happiness.

You may have been through a lot to reach this point, acknowledge and respect your own courage and strength. It is now time to let go of your old stories of wounded suffering to allow your-self to create the life you truly deserve. If you really wish to change your life, only you can create this change. You will need to rewrite your story, to change your energy and to begin creating your own magic, your own beauty, shining your own light, living your love, your way. You have the power, the strength and the ability with love.

Love—I create everything in my existence.

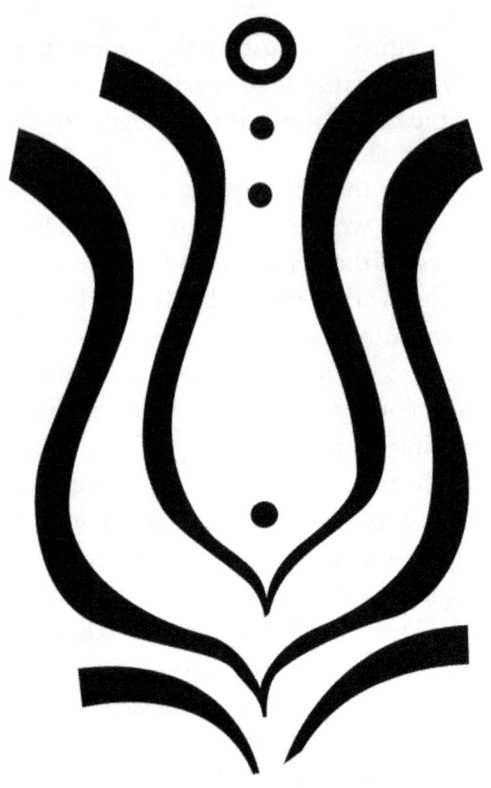

DESERVE THE BEST

You have created your-self in the image of all existence. You do deserve all that you desire. This deserving sense is created through positive loving intention. Expectation and entitlement will only obstruct your creative ability. Connect with your source energy, understand exactly who you are, be your powerful spirit and share your positive, inspirational love with everyone around you. Your shining love will present your universe. As you understand and accept the enormity of your power, you will know the responsibility this entails and you will know how to use your energy for the greater good, not just for personal gain. When you walk your spirit openly, you will change your motivation and methods of living, knowing that while your journey is about your-self, your life is about the entire universe. This may sound grandiose and beyond your comprehension just now although with time and experience, you will know that everything that you do has far reaching influence. If the mere wings of a butterfly can create tidal waves, just imagine what you can achieve.

Through being your spirit, you will feel your connection to all life, its feelings will be your feelings, its suffering will be your suffering, its liberation will be your liberation, connected, all one, evolving together in the one body of all existence. When you create miracles and magic, love and positivity, abundantly and beautifully, sustainably and prosperously, this is the energy you create all around you and right throughout the universe. When you know that your creative ability is not just about your-self, it is the source energy you are meant to share freely and openly to enable and liberate others, you will open your-self to a greater flow of energy than you can imagine. Energy in all its forms is meant to be shared freely and equitably with all souls. We are not meant to accumulate or retain energy as this will create stagnation and imbalance. Just as occurs when a free flowing river is dammed, it will inundate some areas and isolate others. So too does the accumulation of wealth by one restrict the flow of this energy to another. The generation of energy requires effort and when this effort is applied equitably, it will be shared equitably.

Be aware of the seed source of your motivation for all you do, be aware of your connection to all things and know that you are an important element within evolution playing your role with the purity of love as your common intention in all you are. Love just loves, it shares, it compliments, it liberates and it enables others to feel the beauty of its energy. Live your life with this pure intention and you will be rewarded all the riches and love the universe has invested within you.

Love—I live and deserve the best in my life.

ABUNDANCE AND PROSPERITY

All the abundance and prosperity of the universe is within you. Your poverty consciousness, insecurities, sense of lack, that something is missing, your insatiable black hole all exist within you. We spend considerable effort and time striving throughout our lives searching for this energy outside of ourselves only to come to the conclusion that our answers have been within us all along. Too often we become misguided and confused that abundance and prosperity are just about the physical world. We think that when we have all the money, power, possessions, position and people around us, then we will have life made and be successful. This is the desire of most western societies and what a dream this is or is this really the nightmare? Materialism presents an illusion of happiness and there is considerable evidence that money does make us happier or more content. It is true that when you are struggling just to survive, you will do just about anything to survive.

We have created societies of great physical abundance although I feel that we have lost sight of what is really important for sustaining our soul's energy. It is challenging for us to stay connected to the true nature of ourselves when you are living in large, overcrowded and busy cities, doing demeaning work, not knowing love, just existing from one day to the next, without real meaning or intent. Our physicality is our means of expression and experience of our soul's energy. Living a life devoid of spirit is just a life partially lived, empty, meaningless and loveless for everything else is temporary and transitory. Everything in life emerges and passes, lives and dies. All energy, including your lovely money, will pass through your life on its way to its destiny. Our humanity requires consistency and continuity, stability and conformity whereas our spirit thrives on change, flow, spontaneity, creativity, love and imagination. There is a balance to be found here and when you have found your equilibrium, you will be living the truth of your spirit in this human form.

In living your spirit, you will experience all the abundance and prosperity of both spiritual and physical energy in all aspects of your life. Please do not interpret or feel that it is wrong to be affluent or wealthy for this too is your destiny as the powerful, creative, loving soul that you are. You do deserve the best of life to be the best that you can be in this lifetime. Anyone who is aspiring to less than this has not fully accepted the truth of their loving creation. Allow your energy to be free to express all of your-self and share your abundance and prosperity with everyone you encounter. You will know that as you share, you will receive and so on your flow will continue. When you set your soul free, you will also enable others to find their way to share this same freedom and pass this loving energy on. All souls incarnation deserve the best, to enjoy great abundance and to feel real love in their lives.

Love—I create great abundance and prosperity in all that I am.

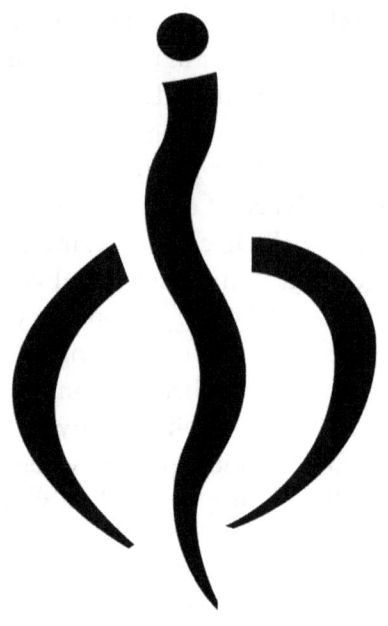

RELAX

The ability to accept everything life presents to you and to be able to relax into flowing with your energies intention is a great gift. As a species that needs to control everything in its influence, most of humanity struggles with this concept, even on the spiritual plane. We think that we are superior beings capable of anything we put our minds to. On one level this is correct however this is generally in the negative sense. You do not have to look far to find the evidence to support our destructive negative ability to control everyone and everything on this planet. Never before have we got it so wrong, war and terrorism, mass extinctions and destruction, global warming, starvation, financial excess and ruin, over population, isolation, poverty and loneliness are the price we pay for losing sight of what life is really about.

Most of us work all year or all of our useful lives striving to create a nest egg to enable us to afford a holiday or even eventually retire only to arrive at this destiny too tired or worn out to enjoy the fruits of this hard labour. Life is not a life sentence. There is more to life than work, acquiring more possessions and how you appear to everyone around you. Once you have physically achieved more than you ever imagined, if you have not connected with your spiritual roots, you will still feel like something is missing. The key to living a happy and meaningful life is to find your purpose, your reason for being and then allow your energy to flow toward this destiny. We all dream of living our dream life, awaking each morning to doing what we love, being in the flow and feeling lovingly alive in every moment. The key to realising your dreams is to take action that is consistent with the outcome you desire.

Everyone here has a purpose to fulfil. There is no escaping your role and you will only get to rest when you complete your destiny. If you think you can drop out or retire without engaging your spirit, you may just find that you will repeat this process until you know and accept the energy of who you really are. To find real relaxation in your life, let go of the need to control your-self and your energetic flow. Tune into your feelings to find your truth and be prepared to be totally honest with your-self. Be present in the moment you are in and face your life as it appears before you. Deal with what you know to be true, focussing on what you feel and do not allow your energy to be distracted by the drama of another. You are just responsible for your-self and your responses to life. Your sense of self, being calmly aware are indicators that you are within you. This is when you know you are in control of your-self and your emotions and you will be in a position to look after your-self and all others. Happiness, relaxation and contentment are the wonderful fruits of the work you have done to free your-self. You will experience more of these beautiful energies as you become even more aware of how you wish to live and love. Just remember that life is in the flow, you just need to relax, let go and flow with your life.

Love—I relax in every experience knowing all is perfect.

SURRENDER

While our life and spiritual journey have order, history and structure, they are dynamic energies of evolution, ever changing, shifting and manifesting in new and challenging forms. Each generation of souls confronts new experiences and change in their own way. Sometimes we will create new and unique ways of dealing with these challenges although most of the time we just continually try to re-solve these issues with the same energy that created the problem in the first place. It is amazing that such clever people can repeatedly experience history without ever seemingly considering the alternatives. This I have never understood. Why do we always choose conflict, hardship and pain as our evolutionary catalyst? It would seem that we have been doing this since the cave and only the weapons and words we use have become smarter. We destroy and harm when we should be nurturing and loving each other. When we attack one another, we only harm ourselves.

We seem to think that if we give in or give up to any form of tyranny or violence that we are weak and giving our power away. True there are times when you need to take care of your-self and your country. Over the last half century, we have all loved the intention of John Lennon's song "Imagine", singing along beautifully with its peaceful melody, although how few of us really live with this energy and belief in our hearts. The "Age of Aquarius" Flower Children became the Corporate Kings of today. We are all living on the same finite evolving planet in the greater body of all existence. We are totally dependent on each other and our actions affect all others in both the positive and negative sense. It is time that we put aside our differences, prejudices, history, traditions, boundaries and beliefs to find our way to living in greater peace and harmony for the collective good of everyone. In order to achieve any resemblance of this intention, all of us need to find this space within ourselves, put aside our insecurities and hunger for power to start living with pure loving intention in all that we are. World peace may be a mighty call; however inner peace is very achievable.

This does require you to surrender your individualised idea of life to know and connect with all the energy of the universe that you are. It is interesting that we can even conceive that individually and separately that we are somehow more powerful than the universe. When you surrender to the energy of the universe that you are, you will know that you are very powerful energetically and that you will only ever use this power with loving, positive intention. You are a vital element of all existence in your space in its flow. Let go of the need to control and manipulate your energy, surrender to where your energy wants to take you and you will find that your life will begin to flow smoothly and beautifully on its course. If you find your-self in hardship, struggle and stress, you will know that you have gone against your own flowing energy. Let go of whatever you are holding onto and to let your energy flow again. We can only imagine our soul's capability and dream about our life's creation. Believe me, when you let your soul be free, your life will turn out more magically and magnificently then you could ever dream. You cannot design or control it, just surrender to your love.

Love—I surrender in my flow.

LET LIFE BE

Your life has its course to run when you let go of your need to control every aspect of it. You have control over how and where you choose to live your life however you do not have control over anyone or anything around you. Your energy is just one element surrounded and influenced by everything you encounter in your environment. Every other soul you meet and the experiences you have, shape and form you. Your programming and conditioning from your family, education, work and play in this and every lifetime have developed you into who you are today. You have made many choices that have brought you to this moment of realisation, every decision perfect in its own time and made without the greater picture in view.

This is life. Observe nature and everything that makes up this beautiful planet we live in and you will see the random inter-connectedness of all life, including your own. Everything individually has its role to play intrinsically linked to all life around it. We are not separate to or superior to any other form of life. In fact we are just as dependant on the health of the planet and all other life as they are reliant upon us. We have taken far too long to accept our responsibilities for our own health and for the negative impact we have had on our planet. You can also see that the poor health of the planet is reflective on our health as a species. While we have made many advances with technology and medical science, our individual health is getting worse, life quality and value have not really improved, we just exist for longer. Prolonging life at any cost is not evolution. We fear death, live unsustainably, devoid of real love, becoming increasingly obsessed by technology and have greater mental and emotional instability due to our unbalanced, unhealthy lifestyles.

Each of us has a responsibility to ourselves to be healthy of spirit, mind and body in order to live sustainably on this earth. When you are connected with your spirit all of your life will flow. You will let go of the need to control your-self and all others and you will flow with the energy of your spirit's intention. Your life will treat you as well as you treat it. Be aware of how you are living and the impact that you are having on those around you and upon the environment. Ensure that your actions are doing no harm to your-self or anyone or anything else and you will benefit directly from this intention. For as you are your life will be. When you live and love positively, it is amazing just how much life has to offer you in return.

Love—I am in the flow of my life.

SERENITY

The peaceful grace of serenity can only be experienced in the flow of your soul's journey. You will be quiet, still and relaxed in your mind, flowing smoothly, creating your magic easily and feeling real love for you in every moment. In the stillness of each moment you will feel serene and in harmony with your life. You will have let go of struggle and stress in every aspect of your life. Your inner peace will reflect in all of your life. Hardship and pain will be replaced with ease and happiness. You will feel relaxed, conscious and at ease within you. You will no longer create drama and conflict as your means for evolution and you will find loving, positive ways of resolving any issue that arises in your life. If you are ever in doubt, look for the loving answer and you will find your way back to your peace. Love is your key.

Whenever you become forgetful, distracted or confused, just remember that the essence of your-self is always at peace and serene. Your quiet peaceful centre will be momentarily interrupted and overcome by the discord created by your negativity and fear. The essence of your-self is found within the stillness of each moment, in the quiet serenity of space. You will know you have lost your sense of self when you do not feel at peace and serene in your being. When you feel out of sorts, be with your-self, listen quietly and mindlessly to the soft eloquence of your truth and you will find answers to any question you pose. This process cannot be intellectualised, forced or constructed, it must be felt. If you are not in tune with or understand your true feelings, you will be continually challenged in finding serenity and peace.

Listen to your pure feelings, surrender to flow with them and allow your life to unfold before you. Serenity is found at the very centre of our being, it is the essence of who you are. When you are within your-self and aware of everything that is going on within you and around you, you will be serene and you will feel it. Through being in this centre, you will not lose this feeling nor will you allow anyone else to distract or pull you from this peace. You will be serenely at peace even when the world around you seems to be spinning out of control. When you know your-self, you will not be caught up in the dramas and issues of others. It is amazing how more productive and constructive you will become as you will not waste your energy on anything that does not honour or serve your soul's evolution. You are peace and serenity, love and light, honour and truth, all you have to do is remember to be your-self.

Love—I am serene and at peace with all existence.

FLOW WITH LIFE

Your energy will always be flowing towards your destiny whether you are aware of this movement or not. Your soul's energy never stagnates or out of its flow, it is always evolving regardless of your state of mind. Your soul is far more aware than you can ever know, it observes and knows all, it experiences and feels all, it is highly sensitive and receptive, it is always connected to universe even if you are not. It does not sleep, take time out or waste its time and energy. The sooner you acknowledge who you really are, the sooner you will connect with this flow and access the universal energy within you. You are meant to flow with your energy, easily and smoothly, just allow you to flow freely and lovingly.

As your spirit is in constant movement, you just need to feel your place in this flow, let go of your reservations and doubts to flow beautifully and magnificently toward your destiny and purpose. Whenever you are out of this flow, struggling or in stress, these are your indicators that you have lost or forgotten your way. Seek another way, look for your alternatives, feel for your loving and positive response in any situation you create. You will find that your life energy will flow more smoothly with less friction and conflict. With practice you will develop your spiritual skills and attributes to a point where acting with love and positivity will be natural and instinctive. You will not have to make any special effort; you will just feel for your answer and then express the truth of your heart in all instances. When you reflect on who you were in the past, this being may seem like a stranger or foreign to you. Your past is not your present unless you are still living in this past. All of your previous experiences have brought you home to your spirit, however you are not meant to continually live your life through any extension of your history.

Life is meant to be easy. Where have you heard that before or haven't you received this message yet? Most of us have been raised on the hard work ethic, the hard luck struggle, never having enough of whatever, life is a bitch and then you die, you know your story. You will have your own little subliminal saboteurs deep inside your psychic. You do not need to seek them out; you just need to acknowledge that you are not the sum of your negative, fearful programming, choices or experiences. With the ultimate power of your consciousness, you can change any program or memory simply by changing your choices and your perspective. You cannot change any past event or circumstance. However you do have the power to change how you remember and perpetuate this energy within you. To remain attached to or consumed by your wound, pain, hurt, memory, pattern, belief or any other negativity is a continual choice. When you let go of your fears and your pain, you will let go of your past releasing your-self to relish the creation of this present moment anew. Whenever you are stuck in the past or dreaming of the future, you will be out of the present moment. The only moment you can change is right now. To make positive changes in your life, this is your moment to change. Be here, flow and create with love and all spirit will present itself beautifully to you.

Love—I am flowing with all life.

LOVE AND TRUTH GUIDE YOU

Awareness of your spiritual nature requires you to walk between love and truth to create your smooth energetic flow. You need to understand and accept all aspects of your-self to be able to really know and love all of your-self. Your truth will be universal, will be honourable and will always be love. The journey you have undertaken to find your truth may not have always been smooth, loving or honourable. However when you have learnt your lessons and let go of anything that has restricted your spirit, you will know from your own experiences, what your life is about and how you need to live from here on. Anything you have learnt theoretically, been taught by another or read will develop your intellectual knowledge. Your actual experiences of life will be engrained and enshrined within your innate knowing. Intellectual knowledge can be swayed through sound, persuasive argument. Your knowing of what you have experienced and felt within your-self cannot.

Your knowing of your soul's experience is your truth and this knowing does not require proof, agreement or validation from anyone else.

Standing in the love of your truth provides you with the inner courage and strength to always remain true to your path. Whenever you concede or compromise your-self to please or satisfy another's need to be right, you will stray from your path and pay your price for not honouring what you know to be true for you. Make this mistake often enough and you will learn eventually. Mistakes are just choices poorly made without sufficient information or awareness to make better, more loving decisions. When you are more conscious of your life, your values and your truth, you will not stray far before you become aware that you have traded off some of you and you will quickly find your way back to your core. Whenever you find your-self in fear, negativity, pain and suffering, you know that you have forgotten your-self and you will come back to you to find your positive, loving answers and solutions. Once again with practice, this will become an easier and less painful process than you have experienced previously.

Be the love and truth of who you are and your life will flow wonderfully and beautifully onto its destiny. You deserve to fully experience this aspect of your-self and to enjoy the fruits of your own creation. You are a powerful all knowing being of pure light, love and truth, at peace within your-self and all others, compassionate, considerate and connected to all existence. Imagine a world where we are all living our love in all that we do and you will commence this process of creation. I can clearly see a time in this physical world where we are all conscious of living our spiritual truth with everyone living bountifully, lovingly, at peace and harmoniously sharing their energy freely and responsibly for the mutual benefit of all existence.

Love—I always walk in my love and truth.

JOURNEY INTO COMPLETENESS

Believe it or not, you are complete and whole just the way you are. All you have to do is accept all of your-self, the beautiful magnificence of the pure love, light and truth of who you are. All your experiences of your creation have illustrated your ability to manifest energy in your life. Should your power be misguided or misdirected by focussing on the negative, fearful aspects of life, then this will be the energy and experience you have created for your-self. Unfortunately until we know better, we will continually create drama and trauma in our lives for our evolutionary growth. Accept that you exist at the centre of all your experiences and you are the only common denominator in everything you have grown through in this life. You are a powerful creator with all the energy of the universe within you, accept this truth and you will know the real power of your-self and you will know how you should focus this energy.

Utilise this vital essence of your-self to discover and remember all of who you are to know your purpose in this life. You are here for a reason that is known only to you and you will need to fully understand how you manifest and generate your energy to know your purpose. Your answers are not outside of you, nor does another know your whole truth. We can show the way, guide you and inspire you. However you possess the key to knowing your-self. When you release your—self imposed shackles and limitations, you will know all of you. During your inner journey, you will need enormous patience, perseverance and persistence inspired by loads of nurturing love. This is a journey that most seek although only a few dare to be different and undertake for real. For too often we let our fears, obligations and conformity stand mythically in the way, only to pay the ultimate price of ignorance for this procrastination.

Step through the thin veil of your illusionary fears, strip away any energy that has held you in the stagnation of comfortable numbness and be adventurous of spirit. You are far more capable than you could ever dream if only you would allow all of you to express and be your spirit. All of your-self is necessary and there is nothing you have ever accomplished in this or any life that has been wasted or is not useful. When you bring all parts of your-self together, combining all of your skills and gifts into your own uniqueness, you will know your way and why you are here. With complete balance and harmony of spirit, mind and body, you will experience serenity and stillness in your heart knowing that you are on your path, honouring and loving all of your life. This is the truth of who you are and why you are here. Be whole within you and your search will end and your creation will really commence in earnest.

Love—I am complete as I am.

ENLIGHTENED JOURNEY OF THE SOUL

This is your journey of light, love and truth, are you having fun yet? Have patience for you soon will. Your path is meant to be joyous, loving, simple, real, magical and wondrous. The truth of who you are is at the centre of your universe that is within you. Come back to your core, in the balance and harmony, pure and simple and you will know that you have found your middle road. The truth does not exist in the dogma of the extremes in whatever form they manifest. Ecstatic highs and desperate lows are inter-related energies created to balance each other out. The lower the lows, the higher the highs will need to be overcome this imbalance and the extreme highs will soon be balanced by your lows. These perpetually extreme movements frequently pass briefly through the centre of the balanced stillness we are all seeking, however we seldom allow ourselves to experience this balance. The truth of your peace, balance and harmony exists in your centre, in your moments of conscious stillness, when you are at peace and feeling whole within you.

When you remember and integrate the truth of your love, light and truth in all of your life, you will live energetically from your core, knowing your purpose and loving every experience you create. You will know that every moment of your awareness is showing you the way, guiding and influencing you to enhance your spiritual life skills. It is true that the more you understand, you will discover how much more there is to know. Do not be alarmed or discouraged for our very limited intellects struggle to conceptualise infinity. It is not necessary to know it all for that would just take a lot of the fun and mystery out of our journey of self discovery. All you really need to know like any good student of life; is to know where your answers are to be found and to know how to access them. This is your connection to the universal truth that you are and this is where you will know what your life is about and that is what is important.

The best example of your spirit you can provide the planet is by living the truth of your love in all that you are in every moment. Lead the change you seek by being who you are regardless of where you are. Shine your light on all you touch and share with. You may not feel that you are having an impact of any consequence; however the difference you are making will be profound and everlasting. When you walk in the truth of your soul, you are nurturing not only your soul; you are nourishing the soul of all existence. This is an awesome responsibility that provides real clarity of purpose and will benefit many lifetimes to come. You are making an energetic investment that will precede all that you encounter and experience. As you magnify and intensify your light, you share this light with everyone and everything around you without effort, it just happens simply by being your-self.

Love—I walk in the light of my love.

MOTIVATION

We often seek encouragement and reasons to take action from outside of ourselves, looking for something or someone to inspire and motivate us to change and improve our lives. It is easy to blame and hold others responsible for your life, whether you are using your family situation, upbringing, education, poverty, traumas or accidents, work, injuries or illness as reasons or excuses for how you live. If this approach is working for you, then I am really surprised that you have read this far. Living with the familiarity of your wound, sadness and negativity may feel comfortable and known for it has been your point of identification and story for a long time now. The more often we repeat our tale of woe will not dissipate its hold upon us, nor will it allow us to move beyond its dark, far reaching tentacles. You will not improve the quality of your life or find true love and happiness in your life while you still cling to the past in whatever form you may have created.

The only moment and the only person you can change is your-self right now. You are responsible for how you create and experience all of your life and until you take full responsibility, you will remain fixated in your past. At some point we need to draw a line in the sand and state categorically to ourselves that it is time to move on. This will be the time when you begin to acknowledge your own power in taking responsibility to start afresh. If you need to set this intention every day, then do it. Whatever it takes for you to get your life back on track; set your course and initiate action to make these changes real. As you take responsibility for your-self, you will access a greater flow of energy through you and you will be your own inspiration for change. You will reap the benefits for taking positive action quickly and your barometer for this change will be in how you feel. You should be experiencing more peace, contentment, resonance and love of your-self through this process. If this is not your experience, then review if you are still using your fears and negativity for your reasons for being.

Finding the motivational energy to follow your dreams is found in having the dream in the first place. You need to allow your imagination and creativity the freedom to daydream and imagine a reality that really inspires your soul. Can you find a space that you would love to create that would make your heart sing freely every day? Try not to focus too heavily on material or physical possessions or even other people. Focus on the energies, feelings, sensations, experiences, creativity, peace, contribution and consciousness you wish to create in every aspect of your life. If you have no idea of where you are going, any road will take you there. It just helps if you have some point of reference to aim your energy towards, to find the inner motivation to take the action necessary to manifest your pure intentions in this life. The key to your creative ability is love. This requires you to love your-self, love what you are about and loving what you are doing all the time. Find the motivation of love for all you are and let your loving intention be the seed you sow in all you do.

Love—I am motivated with my love.

COURAGE

True courage is found in your ability to allow your-self to become so vulnerable, sensitive and loving, that you could feel the soft flutter of the wings of a butterfly. Your senses, your intuition are highly attuned and refined. When you understand all of who you are, you will clearly know the differences between your own energy and the energy fields of others. People often remark that it takes courage and strength to stand in the truth of who you are. I feel the real courage within those souls who are still dragging themselves kicking and screaming through pain and suffering to remember their truth. Placing your beautiful, all knowing, light and loving soul incarnate into this dense, fearful and negative life form requires enormous courage and conviction of spirit. Experiencing and clearing all of life require immense courage and a strength that only the soul possesses. You will know that this courage comes from knowing you are immortal and infinite, knowing there is nothing your soul cannot handle and there is no situation you will not find your way through to your evolution.

Connect with your spirit and you will access strength beyond your wildest imagination. Utilise this strength to stay true to your-self and true to what you are about. Have true belief and conviction in your dreams and dare to be different for all change is in your hands. Be aware of the impact of your energy on others, draw your intention from within your purity, be motivated from love and positivity and always act honourably for the evolution of all souls. Do not listen to your negative voices of fear, doubt and judgement. You have dealt with these noisy monsters, you have taken back your power from your restrictive mind and you now live your love in all that you do. Be true to you and you will naturally be true for others even if they cannot accept this at that moment. Being different, going against the flow of general consensus requires you to have the courage to live your love for you have tried the alternative and that did not work out for you.

When you live to your full potential there will be those souls who do not or cannot understand given their experiences and state of consciousness and this is okay. You are about changing and improving the quality of your life and if this influences others this will be a bonus of spirit. It does not matter that anyone other than your-self gets you and nor should it. You will know who you are and you will also know more about the human condition as well. If they invite you to share and accept your offerings, that will be great, however this is not essential. As long as you are happy and contented in knowing your-self and you are sharing your love freely and honestly, you are a long way down your path of evolution. You are one of the few brave souls who have found your way and you should acknowledge the courage and strength you have shown in your-self to be where you are. It is truly magnificent and miraculous to re-discover your soul's purpose and to find that it was not as difficult as you were led to believe.

Love—I have the courage and strength of all spirit.

FIND THE JOY IN YOUR HEART

The energy of this symbol is possibly one of the most useful sensory intentions that you will invoke in your life. When I was deep within my own struggle, I asked a spiritual friend how I would know when I was out of my head and in my heart. At the time I was extremely challenged with my life and with understanding this knowing in particular. He quite simply said, "you will know that you are in your heart when you can feel joy regardless of where you are or what you are going through" or words to that effect. I still was not clear with this explanation and just let the words sit with me. A few hours later I was driving home from buying some groceries with tears rolling down my face, laughing my head off saying god I love what I am going through and in that moment, I finally got what he had meant. Out of all the symbols and energy I experienced during this time, this was one of the most profound and obvious moments of realisation I have ever felt and there have been some.

Experience is our greatest teacher as it develops your inner knowing and your unique gifts for dealing with the challenges that you create for your evolution. You will just know when you have your own realisations of your truth. You will know what resonates and feels right for you. Your truth is not contained or developed by your intellectual mind, this facility just records, analyses and files information. Your truth must be felt through your senses, primarily with the pure feelings of your spirit which is accessed through your heart space. If you have not connected with your heart to know the difference between the mind and your heart, you will always be trying to think your way to your truth. You will have some success as there is so much information available on just about everything you would like to know. The only drawback in this approach is that it is intellectual and therefore limited by your programming and conditioning. When you access your heart, your senses, your spirit provides you with access to your universal knowing. Your pure feelings of your heart cannot be programmed or controlled. You will just know through all of your senses that this knowing is far more powerful than anything you have experienced before and that your feelings are right for you.

Take some time in every day to acknowledge your heart, your spirit and you will develop your relationship with your-self and the senses you share. As this relationship grows beautifully and lovingly, you will understand what I am sharing with you. Your heart is the key to who you are and contains all the energy you will ever wish to experience. When you start filling your heart with your pure love of you, you will overflow abundantly with love and know that as you are loving with others, you are really only loving your-self. You can never love your-self too much and implicit in this knowing is that you can never love anyone else too much either as you are just releasing your love to return to you. You are creating, generating and releasing an infinite loop of love to revolve and evolve all around you. Magic happens as you love.

Love—I connect totally with the loving joy in my heart.

LOVE COMPANION

Your motivation and inspiration for all you create should always be love and truth. When you connect with the essence of your soul's energy, you will know the pure intention of your primary feelings in everything you experience. You are pure love, light and truth and you are requested to live the truth of who you really are in every moment of your creation. Be sure to know your core motivation, your reasons and your base intention for all you desire. Your initial feeling of creation is the seed intention you sow in your energy field. If you are fearful, insecure or negative, this will be the seed energy of your desired intention. Regardless of how positive and loving you try to be to overcome your fears, if you have not cleared or cleansed your energy field, you will still be attached to this negativity, therefore attracting more of these experiences into your life. One issue with positive affirmations can be that you are only just positively reinforcing your own fears and therefore amplifying more of these undesired experiences into your life.

It does require effort and discipline on your part to clear your way to your truth. Impulsive and reactionary responses to your environment will not be your answer in these situations. You need to create your-self a quiet space to ponder your situation, your motivation, your values and your intentions. While this process may be initially challenging, with perseverance and practice it will become instinctive and natural. All your behaviours, reactions and thoughts are rooted in our collective programming. When you ultimately decide to take full responsibility for living your own life, you will have the power to change these patterns and conditioned behaviours. This is an integral element of your free will, allowing your-self the choice to be and do things differently and feel at peace with your own choices. It is only when we compromise and erode our sense of self to fit in or belong that we lose touch with who we really are or desire to be.

Find your own motivation and inspiration for living your love and you will know this reality. Being loving and honest with your-self at all times is essential for living your spirit's love. Stay true to your-self and be aware of the triggers for every reaction and response to your environment. When we are reacting from our sub-conscious programming, you will not feel in control or totally aware of your emotions or feelings. You will experience the negative, fearful aspects of your-self through expressing with pain, hurt, anger, rage and victimhood. Master these reactionary outbursts through knowing your spirit self and you will be more aware of each situation, in tune with your feelings and you will respond with more love and compassion even in hostile situations. Do not judge your-self if you still sometimes lose control. There will be times when you need to stand in your power and stand up for what you believe to be true for you. Being spiritual does not mean that you have to become so meek and obliging that you are continually used and abused, this is not love or honourable in any way. It is also true that you can love everyone without necessarily liking how they conduct or present themselves. Connect with your loving self and be love in all that you are and you will experience this love in all of your life. If you do not feel love, then maybe it is time for change.

Love—When I walk with love, I am free to be me.

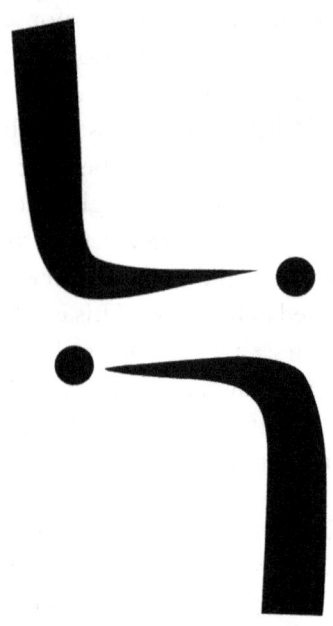

CREATE IN EVERY MOMENT

You have the power of creation within your soul. Who you are is the source of your creation and everything you have experienced in this and every lifetime. You are creative whether you choose to believe this truth or not. From the moment you awaken to the moment you awaken is an infinite stream of creative choices and decisions made by your-self. You may feel sometimes, that all your choices and experiences are not totally your own and this can be true if you have given your power away. However when you strip aside your lame excuses and justifications, you will know deep within your-self, that you have always had choices, you have just not been prepared to accept or conscious of those choices at that time. We all make infinite choices every day. Sometimes they can be hard to make, have an impact on others, trigger our fears and insecurities and require us to take real responsibility for improving the quality of our own lives.

Having the courage to create the life of your dreams can be challenging and difficult to really know what you should do next. Being brave is not the only quality you will need. I found that trust is the bigger issue here, for you need to really trust your inner feelings, your gut instincts that have brought you to this moment. They are real and these feelings have their purpose. They are your access to your creative force. If you are still trying to think your way to your spirit, you will take a lot longer and be more challenged. Feel your way to your creativity, play with it, experiment, explore, dabble or do whatever it takes to disconnect your mind to enable your-self to feel for your truth. In your truth you will find your trust of your-self. The interesting element of trust is that it will only support you for as long as you trust completely. Any doubt or second guessing will set you back until you learn to really trust yourself totally.

In accepting that you are the source of your own experiences, creating and developing your own way of living, you will realise the full power of who you are and you will be able to create innovatively in all that you are. Be aware of the energies and experiences that you are creating in every moment. There has been considerable focus on manifesting and creating materially, vision boards, mission statements and so on. If living your life surrounded by the physical trappings of success is your motivation, I am not here to discourage you. Just be aware of what you wish for. You may just find your manifestation is not connected to or resemble love in any form. Creativity is about the energy you are and the energy you share with your fellow soul travellers, doing all you can to empower everyone around you to live fully and lovingly in all their lives. Your energy is all that you take with you and should you wish to really evolve, you will need to create from this intention and this perspective. I am not judging or damning any physical or material manifestation or attraction laws, just be aware that your seed motivation will create your outcome.

Love—I am the powerful creator of all that I experience.

CLARITY OF SIGHT

Your ability to know your life path exists within your soul's memory. When you connect with the truth and love in your heart, you will access your universal knowing. Allow your-self to imagine, dream, visualise and energetically create your ideal way of living and set your energy free to experience this new reality. Focus on the spiritual or sensual experiences and energy you desire in your life and allow your physical manifestation to follow this intention. Too much focus on your physical life can only create in this very restrictive and transitory material form. When you channel all your creative energy into the purity of your senses and feelings, you will know the truth of these words. The real energy of your experiences will remain true for you forever. As your experiences have an eternal impact on your evolutionary consciousness, any focus on your soul's energy is worth the investment.

Having access to your spirit is not just another skill or qualification you acquire to possess all you desire, to have your own way or to be superior to others. In fact spirituality is quite contrary to just about everything that our modern way of living encourages and rewards. Living from your heart is not about having or obtaining all that you want, it is about letting go for the need of physicality and materialism to live more simply and lovingly in everything we are. When you truly love your-self in every moment, you will know that all the possessions and toys, beauty and fame, position and status, power and might are not about love. These finite aspirations of humanity are quite shallow and fleeting for they will not fulfil the soul and they do not make us feel any better than we have always felt. You will have experienced the facade of this emptiness for your-self and know this to be true.

Come back to all of your-self to really connect with your soul's intention and you will clearly see how you can achieve real fulfilment and contentment in your life. Find the pure love of your-self within you, live this love in all that you are and be who you are really meant to be. Focus on what is important to you, find your inspiration for living your love, channel all your energy into being the best that you can be and always stay true to your intentions. You will know your way. You will immediately know when you have lost or forgotten your way and you will know how to find your way back to you. Life is to be lived in the simplicity and flow of your core energy and you will know when your life style does not feel right for you. Being sensitive and attuned to life all around you is a true blessing and your feelings will always show you the way. Trust what you know to be true even when others are in their doubt and judgement. You do know who you are.

Love—My feelings show me my way.

PATIENCE

Patience is a wonderful virtue. Unfortunately too few seem to have an abundance of this beautiful energy within or around us. We are constantly striving and struggling to be elsewhere, be doing differently, having more stuff, grasping and acquiring, seeking that next fix or revelation or whatever turns you on. Being patient is all about being right here in this moment, content and at peace with exactly where we are and accepting the perfection this moment presents. It is incredible that we rarely experience real patience when it is one of the easiest sensations to achieve. All that is required of you is to be present, be aware of your surroundings and listen quietly for your guidance in its time. Everything can only happen when it does and every moment is in the perfection of your creation. Even though you are a powerful being of pure creation, you are one soul of infinity in the energetic flow of the universe. While your evolution does impact on all universal creation, you are not solely responsible for the transformation of all mankind or the universe. Accept your role is essential and that you are not alone in this evolutionary process. Just let go and come back to your role, be who you are and be the best you can be in this life.

Everything in the universe is always in its divine order and you will always be exactly where you need to be to receive your gift of life. Accept your guidance and your unique gifts and be all you can to live your love fully in all that you are. Patience allows you to flow smoothly and peacefully in all that you do. One step at a time, in pace with your energies flow, liberation and infinity are your sensory indicators that you are where you need to be. When you stray outside of these feelings, you will know that you have gone against your own flow. You do not need to control this flow, it is always in movement, shifting and evolving all energy within and around you. All you need to do is let go and flow with your-self.

When you have real peace, stillness and serenity in all of your life, you will know the essence of patience. You will have accepted the power of your creative genius and you will be living your love in all that you are. Patience will allow you to feel your way, giving you the time and space to create and clearly see your next choice. When you are in this flow of energy, everything will have slowed down and quickened simultaneously, you will be quietly still within any chaos that may be around you, you will create the time to do what you need to do and you will still be looking after your-self in the process. Too often we lose sight of what is really important in our lives, caught up in what is going on around us, trying to influence and control external forces and generally wasting time and energy on issues that do not concern us or cannot change. Bring your focus back onto your-self and your sphere of influence and you will have taken back your power from everyone and everything. With acceptance and patience, you will be living your life at your pace, within your control.

Love—I am patient, accepting all creation is perfect.

HONOUR AND HUMILITY

To live with true honour and humility requires you to be aware of all of your-self. Being able to honour oneself in the presence or service of others is an acquired skill that will take years to polish into your art form. When you are of service or involved with the issues of others, you will need to be aware of your own feelings, learning, patterns or triggers with any similar behaviours, habits or rituals that may still exist within you. All of your life is about you. When you really understand this notion, you will know everything is created in your reality for you to know more about your-self and our collective expression of spirit.

Having real honour means honouring your-self in every moment, being aware of your responses or reactions, fully conscious of your life lessons and listening to all the guidance you are provided. Living in humility is your evidence of how you are honouring your-self. Being really humble is not about postulation or being less than another. Humility is the true essence of your spirit, aware, conscious, confident and authentic in every circumstance. You will be living your life from your spiritual core, free of materialistic, power based posturing, standing tall in the real power of who you are without any egotistical arrogance. Sometimes this confident awareness may be judged by others who are still finding their way through the arrogance of who they are not. Remember, how you judge is a reflection of how you feel or think.

When you know who you are, you will choose your own way of life and you do not need to follow or be followed. You will find the path that is right for you and you will know that some will walk with you for a time and others will not. Try to accept without judgement that you know what is true for you and enable others to be free to explore their own truth. You have incarnated to be all of your spirit in this physical body and this is the only truth that you really need to remember. Your spirit knows the way; it is always with you and connected to the entire universe. Walk your path smoothly and harmlessly, always with truth and love in your heart, conscious of all your feelings and how you share your energy with others. You are here to experience all of this life, joyously in celebration of the magnificent creation that your spirit is. As you honour your life, you honour the lives of all others. Be humble and circumspect in how you present your energy, you do not need to preach or judge others, just be who you are and you will know what is right for your spirit.

Love—I live with honour and humility in all that I am.

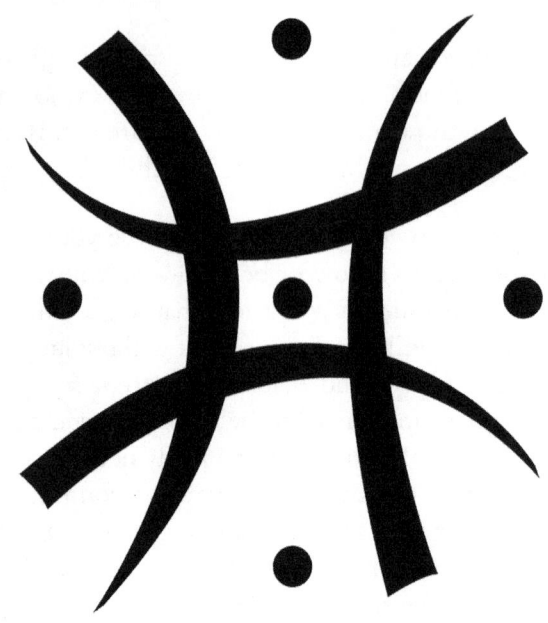

SACREDNESS

All life is sacred. Your life, how you are living, the people you are sharing your journey with, your environment, the planet and all existence are vital elements of the one inter-connected body of all there is. There is no separation or isolation in the universe, everything is inclusive, connected and impacts on everything. To illustrate this connection simply, every cell, every atom, every molecule that constitutes your physical body is the same energy that exists right throughout the universe. Should a cell within your body harm itself, it will affect every cell within the universe; this is the impact of your energy. When you repair and heal your-self, clearing your energy field of all negativity and fear, this inner work has a far greater and positive impact on all life. This is why you are sacred as part of the whole and it is important that you realise who you really are.

We are all searching for greater meaning and purpose for this life although few of us achieve our goals. One of the reasons behind this shortcoming is that our objectives are frequently physically oriented without any spiritual foundation or inspiration. When you have materially acquired all that you lusted after, you will still obsess and desire more and more until you have exhausted your-self, those around you and the precious resources of this beautiful planet. Through understanding that you live and love within the greater body of all there is, you will realise that a physical life focussed on short term, single lifetime oriented goals is quite empty and narrow sighted. As there are no pockets in a shroud, you will take no-one or nothing with you except your consciousness into your next incarnation. At sometime during your life you will come to this realisation and begin to create your own reasons for being here. When you start asking these questions, you will respect the sacredness of your life.

This physical life is truly a sacred gift of our spirit. You have incarnated to integrate your spirit within your physical body to be the best that you can be in this lifetime. You have an important role to play when you fully comprehend why you are here and you will show your way by living your truth in all that you are. You are sacred, you are open, you are love, you are all knowing and you are fully connected to all the energy of the universe. If you are still questioning or doubting your spiritual gifts, reflect on what is really holding you back and you will find that it will not be your spirit, it can only ever be your humanity. Your spirit will always liberate, simplify, enhance and encourage your aspirations. You are totally creative and loving in every way. Feel the real power of your-self and you will know how sacred you and all others are.

Love—Life is sacred.

BLESSINGS

You are truly blessed with the divinity of your soul in every moment of your life. You are divine creation of pure love in this physical form whether you have fully experienced this reality in your life or not. You have been blessed and guided by spirit in all that you have created and experienced. Have you ever wondered how you have made it this far, in those moments of self doubt and despair, when you thought that you could not survive, never mind thrive throughout your life. You have gifts, strength and energetic connections beyond your wildest imagination and you have the ability to overcome and prosper through every experience you create. There is nothing in the universe that you cannot create and there is no experience you can create, that you cannot grow through to be more of the spirit that you are. It is interesting that most of us only relate to our spirit when times are hard, chaotic or disastrous without really acknowledging what this means. As a species, we are yet to learn simply, easily and joyously without all the pain and suffering of our ancestors.

Each of us has enormous responsibility to invoke the power of our spirit, to begin living our lives with love and truth as our motivation for all that we create. It is only then that we will fully embrace the blessedness of this life and have all the blessings of this bountiful paradise bestowed upon us. Each of us has our moments in the darkness, questioning, abusing, doubting, accusing and denying our spirit. We experience the power of our negative fears through the evidence of this energy all around us every day. You have infinitely greater power to create lovingly and positively should you choose a different way. There is no-one in your way other than your-self. All you have to do is to get out of your own way and set your spirit free to be who you really are. The amazing gift you will receive will be really living with awareness and feeling truly blessed in all of your life. When you start to treat your life well, your life will treat you in kind.

By living consciously you will know that you have been blessed right throughout your life. You may not have received everything that you have ever wanted although you would have been blessed with everything that you needed to reach the next stage of your journey. It is not important that you have what you want or desire. It is important that you want and really appreciate what you have and acknowledge how blessed and sacred you are. Everything in all existence is here to support and nurture you in its divine order. You can only be where you are, look around you and embrace all the gifts that you currently have with you and just take one moment at a time. You will find your way to greater peace and harmony in your life; it is just a matter of trust and staying true to you. All of your life, the essence of your love, your unique gifts, and the infinite expression of your energy are truly blessings of life. Embrace them, enjoy and celebrate your love and be your-self.

Love—I am blessed.

HOLY TRINITY

This symbol is powerful in enabling you to directly connect with your higher self, your access to all the energy of the universe within you. When you connect with this source energy of your spirit, you will have access to all the spiritual knowing you will ever require. The Holy Trinity of Spirit exists within all your body, mind and soul through your feminine, masculine and child energies in this physical form. As you grow more aware of how you present your energy and how your soul materialises in this physical form, you will attune to the essence of your spirit. The whole universe is within you, the source code in the Akashic Records, the memory of all existence is hard wired within your DNA, your soul memory. As you connect with more of your-self and accept this is really who you are, you will find that you feel and know more about life than you have ever learnt or experienced.

It is okay for you to listen for your own answers and for you to apply your wisdom in your own way. Too often we become fearful of being different, ostracized and judged by others. It is now time to step into all of who you really are. We all have access to the same information and spiritual knowing. Your interpretation and assimilation of your energy will be unique to you. There is no one else quite like you nor should there be. You have been uniquely moulded by all of your experiences into the special expression of spirit that you are. It would be highly unlikely that there would be another infinite soul shaped exactly as you have been. Therefore it is right to be the uniqueness that is your-self, to find your own way to present your truth in the form that has worked for you. For too long we have all given our power away to others who seemingly know more than ourselves only to find that their way doesn't quite work out for you. You will also experience this with your gift, for what works for you will not necessarily always ring true for others.

Connect with the spiritual trinity that is your-self and explore all of who you really are. If this initially feels strange or odd to you, this is a good indication that you are on your own path, making your choices of truth, experimenting and testing your own life philosophies. The periphery of your reality is generally where all the great ideas and unique concepts are found. You will find common beliefs and ideas through association and subscription to group thinking. It is rare to find real gems in the main stream. Dare to be different, go against the flow of consensus thinking and explore fresh, unique ideas that may just present a new, more effective way for us to live better lives together. We all have a duty to be who we really are and to be all of our spirit in our everyday lives. You just have to ask your-self, are you ready to be your spirit wherever you are.

Love—I connect with my spirit in every experience.

BRING YOUR SELF TOGETHER

Our collective spiritual journeys are varied and unique. You have come to your realisations in your own way, in your own time. The experiences, dramas, traumas and adventures you have created in every lifetime have been your own, each one, each moment leading you right to this moment. You have acquired many skills, talents, attributes, habits, rituals and behaviours that make up who you really are. Everything you have ever learnt; experienced or felt is still within you, creating the vibration that is your consciousness. This vibration influences where you incarnate, the lessons you have to learn and therefore determines the quality of each life. Each soul has its own vibration frequency resonating with similar frequencies to attract the experiences that will ensure your evolution as a being of pure consciousness. We tend to question this process too intellectually instead of utilising our spiritual curiosity to delve deeper into our soul memory. There is also a tendency to remain stuck in our experiences or our wounds when we are required to heal and move beyond these limiting, painful experiences. Your pain is not your comfortable partner, it is the energy you have utilised to amplify and accelerate your evolution. I encourage you to befriend and even love whatever discord or disease you have created to commence your healing process. This loving energy will activate your evolution into the magnificent being of pure light and love that you already are.

Upon realising that there is more to life than what we have been physically taught to believe, many of us disassemble every aspect of our lives, stripping ourselves bare to the point where you no longer recognise who you are. This process is often necessary to renovate and reinvent our souls. We need to undo and release any old armour or defences, heal and clear any psychological or emotional wounds, repair and reconstitute our bodies, examine and retest our belief systems and programming. This is an ongoing process, requiring commitment and perseverance to observe and reflect on every aspect of life. Use your strong intellect and even more powerful intuitive skills to review and determine how your life should be. You may have made some poor judgements or ill informed decisions however this is all part of the process of trial and error of the soul. You will have grown through really living your life, possibly for the first time. While we are all perfect, created in the image of the supreme creator, we are living imperfection, striving to integrate our beautiful, loving spirits into these dense, fear ridden, heavily programmed physical bodies and we wonder why we have struggled.

You are magnificent just the way you are. Accept and acknowledge that you are perfect and whole right now. You have been through the mill and back, you have disassembled and reconstituted your-self, you have explored and trialled many ways of being, you have discovered your own uniqueness and you have attempted to live your truth. It is time for you to bring all of your-self together, form a long lasting and loving relationship with all aspects of your-self to be the best you can be in this lifetime. You have always known what you need to do; it is now time to take action with your knowing.

Love—I am complete and whole as I am.

EMBRACE CHANGE

Always remember that you cannot change and remain the same. The only constant in life is change. All energy, all time, all life, all the universe is in constant movement, growth and contraction, expansion and evolution. You are a vital part of this change and your enlightenment contributes towards the evolution of all existence. Any forgetfulness or negativity pollutes and constricts not only your growth; this contamination is also experienced throughout the universe. While we may feel insignificant in the greater scheme of things, you are part of this whole body and can make a real impact with your life. You have already created powerfully. Reflect on all your negative experiences so far and the role you played in their creation. You now have the opportunity to create your dream life, let go of all your fears and yourself limiting behaviours and habits. Accept that you are the change you wish to create and commence being the person you would love to be in every moment. It is true that you may not always get it right. All change requires a faithful leap into the unknown, stepping outside your comfort zone and requires you to be different.

Change is your friend and ally for it is fresh, creative and energetic. What have you noticed in your moments of apathetic stagnation and comfortable melancholy? During these times how did you feel, how comfortable, inspired and alive were you? The longer you spend in comfortable lethargy, the less likely you are to take risks, to want to change and the more everything will stay the same, comfortable numbness. If this is working for you, you do not have to change. However I would suggest that you are not as content as you would like to believe and it is only your fears and lack of self belief that are holding you back. Take a chance, walk through the tissue thin illusion of your fears and you may just find that the obstacles you have placed before you are not as solid or difficult to move through than you thought. You deserve to live a loving, happy, prosperous and energetic life. All you really have to do is to set this intention and follow your energy towards your spirit's destiny.

Take one step at a time, feel your way, follow what is right for you and always remain true to your-self. The possibilities presented in change are infinite, positive and loving to you. Change is not threatening, restrictive or fearful. You have so much potential for growth and expansion when you accept your spirituality. Life will not be the same nor should it be. You have set your course to really start living and this is when you will begin to really feel all of life. Your feelings are your barometer, your guidance and your true soul compass. Listen to your pure feelings in every moment and you will know what you need to create next. Take your time, move at the pace that suits you and always remain true to you. You are the individual who is creating and experiencing your change, be conscious of the impact your choices have on others and create no harm or mischief along your way. The seeds you sow will be your life harvest. Lay down your positive and loving intention and allow your energy to flow beautifully along your path.

Love—I embrace and prosper through change.

SENSE OF PURPOSE

Every being of pure creation is seeking greater purpose and direction in their lives. Generally we are waiting for some guidance or insight from wiser souls when this innate sense exists inside all of us. Only you can know your way. Others may be able to provide you with guidance and direction. However they cannot walk your path for you. Just as I can provide you with insights into my journey and the path I have taken, this has been my path, it may not necessarily serve you. You always need to listen to your-self, assimilate your energy field and take on only the guidance that feels right for you. We are meant to walk our own paths in our truth. We are not meant to assemble, congregate, subordinate or lessen our souls in any form. You can share and test your energy field with others, however always be aware of your own energy and the clarity you are providing. We are here to be the best that we can all be, unique, energetic and free in every way. You will know when you are with other light hearted souls for they will share themselves freely as you do.

It is important that you constantly review where you are at and what you are doing for it is easy to lose your way when you are not paying attention. Being aware requires you to consciously walk your path in every moment. There are no accidents or chance occurrences. Everything has its purpose of creation and when you are aware of this, you will be conscious that all of life is showing your way. Every situation, every interaction, every sign, every experience is creating you. We create life with every choice, every decision we make. Creativity is not just about artistic achievement. All of life is creative. So take time to focus your intention, to dream your possibilities, to visualise your ideal life and set your love on its course. This is a continual process of re-creation and renewal for as you change, so too will your energy, perspective and intention. You can only know when you know. Therefore, your truth will be in constant evolution just as you are. Nothing is static.

Your aspirations for this life should be monumental and significant. Your spirit is completely free, loving, positive, honest and creative and you are only ever limited by your physical emotional self. Learn to listen to your heart's desire. Differentiate between your head's physical needs and desires versus your heart's energetic loving intentions, for they may not be connected. Your heart may struggle to follow your physical achievements. However your physical needs will always be fulfilled by your heart desires. The physical will always follow the energy you create and this is not always possible in reverse, otherwise we would all be evolved right now. Listen clearly and intently to your feelings, find the love in your creation, seek the positivity in your aspiration and then set your energy free to follow this path. Your life is your creation of experience. Take charge of your creation of life and you will change your destiny.

Love—I create my purpose in this life.

CREST OF CHANGE

We live in interesting times of pure evolution where many long held belief systems and processes are being questioned, challenged and obliterated. The whole planet is going through a process of accelerated evolution, time is quickening and the process of life is changing before our eyes. Technology is being embraced like never before, there is more information available at all levels of society, redundant structures and belief systems are under threat, religious extremism underpins most conflict and there is more psychological dysfunction than ever before. This is the modern society we have created for ourselves, everyone working harder and longer, consuming everything in our paths and in the process slowly destroying our gorgeous life-giving planet. We have developed such a short sighted, narrow-minded view of the world, living for the day, using and abusing all our valuable resources (including our human potential) and in some cases without any real spiritual or value based code to live by.

It is unfortunate that many individuals feel powerless to have a positive impact on this degradation and this could not be farther from the truth. You do have the power to change your world and how you live your life. All you have to do is take full responsibility for the conscious creation of your life and that is it. You do have the innate power to change your life in any moment. There are no excuses or valid reasons for you not to take charge of your life. When you are considering any change, be aware that every choice has consequences and can impact on others. Be sure you are clear with your intentions, of why you are making each choice and be considerate of the consequences you may create. While you are not responsible for the journey of another, you will have energetic connections with other souls that will need to be healed and resolved. Otherwise this karmic bondage will continually play out until you release or heal this energy within you.

When you are facing the critical changes in your life, be careful not to be consumed or overwhelmed by this change. It is so easy to lose sight of your choices and to be swamped by the upheaval you have created. Take a deep breath, regain your perspective and create the space for you to deal with each circumstance in its divine order. There is nothing that you create in your reality that you do not have the ability to walk through. Have true courage in your convictions, stay true to your path, be kind and loving to your-self and others every step of the way. You are a pure being of love and light, it is just a matter of remembering who you really are.

Love—I am loving change.

CHOICES OF LIFE

You always have choices. Every choice is of your creation. These choices will either be made automatically from your physical programming or from the consciousness of your spirit. Every decision you have ever made in every lifetime has created your soul memory manifesting in the life you are currently experiencing. If this seems a little daunting, consider your current life and reflect on how you have created thus far, then multiple this impact over many lifetimes and you will understand your creative role. By taking responsibility for your creation, you will become aware of how and why you make the choices you have. With awareness, you can change your consciousness and the quality of your life. In the past you may have given away your power to the wisdom or control of others or feel that you were not free to choose your own way. Regardless of your situation, you always have choices and choosing to stay where you are is still a choice. I know that it takes real courage and strength to change your circumstances and I also know that you have what it takes to grow and prosper beyond where you currently are. We are all far more capable than we believe.

Choosing to walk the path of your spirit will light the way for you to clearly see. Our spiritual programming of the past may have required solitude, contemplation, isolation, suffering, postulation, meditation, practice, prayer, abstinence, penance, chastity, hardship, poverty, dedication and piety. While elements of these age old practices may be effective introductions or reminders of your spirituality, I found structured processes that dictated rigid rules, restraint, limitation or hardship did not resonate well with my spirit. I have distinct memories of these lifetimes and while these practices have brought me to this realisation, I know deep within me that they will not liberate my soul. The spirit I know intimately and wholly is totally loving, honest, positive, enabling, simple, creative and above all free to be all you desire to be. This is the energy I tune into, listen intently to and always act upon. Any messages or processes that are rule based, conditional, restrictive, secretive, fearful or negative have been filtered through our human conditioning and should be considered wisely along with your own awareness.

The real gift of knowing your-self is the intrinsic understanding you develop within you. In knowing all of your-self, you do not require the approval, validation or confirmation of anyone else. You will be okay with your-self just as you are and you will be living the life that honours and loves all of you. This will be your barometer of your truth for if your life is not working for you, you will have the power to change course. Feel for your truth, if something feels right then follow this energy and do not create choices that do not feel right for you. My truth is always loving, honouring, positive and simple for me to act upon and these are the basic elements I use to discern all my choices and advice. There will be times when your choices may adversely affect others. When you honour your heart's intention, you will be honouring the soul of another even though they may not realise this at the time. Just remember to always choose the loving, positive way of life and you will always be your honourable spirit.

Love—I always create with loving choices.

OPENING TO OPPORTUNITIES

Right here, right now there are infinite opportunities all around you if only you will allow your-self to reach out to the possibilities of your spirit. You have the power to create real magic and wonderment in your life now. You may not believe me. Take a moment, empty your thoughts, tune into your feelings and listen quietly for your soul. At first you may not hear much, however with practice and intention, you will. Your spirit will always be here for you, patiently awaiting your attention to present itself. You just need to quieten your busy mind, be at peace and listen to the gentle loving whispers of your soul. You may only receive a word, a picture or image, sound or colour. It is not important what you receive, it is just important that you listen and act upon whatever guidance you feel is right for you.

It will be through this guidance that you will open to your life opportunities that have been hovering around you for most of your life. Have you ever wondered when other people who are not even connected to you, create ideas or concepts that have come to you or you have seen in the past. Ideas, creativity, images, knowing, energy all exist in the ether of life, all floating around looking for a space in which to materialise. We all have this energy around and within us. You do not need to be especially gifted or seemingly talented to access this energy. All you need to do is to act upon your insights by creating from the essence of an idea regardless of how miniscule it first appears. Take the opportunities as they present themselves for you will never know where it will lead you if you do not make these conscious choices. Everything in all existence is guiding and influencing your creation, all you have to do is be aware of your signs and have the fortitude to take action with these ideas.

Accept that you are a powerful being of pure loving creation and this will be your reality. Creativity is not just about creating some form of commerciality or physical outcome. Creativity is about creating life, creating spirit in this physical form, firstly for your own evolution and if it is meant to be shared with the rest of humanity, it will find its way for this to occur. The essence of who you are is creative and when you access your creativity, you access your spirit. By physically creating from your spiritual core, you are expressing the essence of your soul. Be aware when you exhibit your creativity, you will be placing your soul on public display for all to see. You will need to be ready for this very raw exposure, for if you have any unresolved issues or insecurities, these will be amplified and accelerated by this healing process. Take your time and be with your loving evolution. Be aware of all your signs and guidance to receive your energetic creative gift and take the action to fully express all of your spirit in this lifetime. You will be pleased you made the effort.

Love—I deserve, accept and act on all my evolutionary opportunities.

UNIVERSAL ENERGY

All matter, all space, all existence is pure energy and this includes you. Your body, your mind and your spirit are all just energy vibrating at the frequency that creates this physical form. Every cell, every molecule, every atom within your body is just as every soul, every atom, every particle of energy is right throughout the universe. Every cell of energy within your body is implicitly connected and influenced by your state of mind and your mood, connecting your energy field to every soul around you and through all existence. How you feel, think, express and act influences your vibration frequency creating your experience of this life. We are often challenged in taking this level of responsibility for ourselves and our lives. However if you are still blaming or holding others responsible for your life, you will struggle to take back your power and to take control of creating the life experiences you desire.

If you can allow your-self to consider that you are at the centre of your own universe with all other energies, beings and matter spinning around you, you will have some idea of your sphere of influence. How you are, how you feel and how you experience life is unique to you and only ever truly felt by your-self. We all have our own experience of life from our own perspective, programming and incarnation stream. No two souls will travel the same path in the same way, just as no two humans will experience life in the same form. We are all unique within ourselves, sharing our vibration and our gifts in our own way and these are the qualities that make this life so interestingly diverse and rich in experiences. You are an essential element within this existence as you play your role in re-connecting with your-self, with the planet and with all existence.

When you are living with your soul's intention, you will have universal energy running consciously through your body in all you do. Through walking on the planet consciously, you are sharing the regenerative healing properties of the universe with all you encounter. For too long we have ignored our spiritual energy, given our power away to others and relinquished our spiritual direction to religious organisations or wiser souls. Many of us still feel that we do not fit in or will not be accepted by others and that ancient belief systems are still prevalent today. I suggest you take an honest look at your world, observe how well we are living our collective spirituality and ask your-self, what you can create to make a real and positive difference. Every one of us has an important role and when you re-connect with your own spiritual vitality, you will know what your role is. It does not matter what you are doing, although it does matter how you consciously feel when you are doing it. Connect with the universal energy of who you really are and you will know.

Love—I am Universal Energy.

CREATIVITY

Action is the key difference between the lives of people who achieve their life purpose and those still groping around in the dark. It is not enough to have dreams, ideas and aspirations if you are not willing to create the physical effort to bring them into being. Every one of us is entirely creative in every sense. You create your life with every decision and choice that you make. Even when you are sleeping, you are creating your dream world in your super conscious which will also influence the quality of each day. Whether you can accept this truth or not, you are creative and it is time you created your reality with consciousness, rather than being on automatic pilot. You are not a programmable robot or here just to make up the numbers, you are a magnificent creative being of pure love, light and truth. When was the last time you really acknowledged this fact? Remembering who you really are is a critical element of your creative source. Attempt to create purely from your physicality and you will severely restrict the flow of your energy. Create from your spiritual source and you access the infinite energy of the universe that is you.

Allow your-self time to daydream, imagine, visualise and play with ideas and concepts that seem to randomly come to you in the oddest of moments. For when you allow your mind to take time out from all its processing, analysing, critiquing, categorising, judging and endless chatter, your mind will wander and conjure different thoughts and inspirations for you to explore. While the well trodden path is down the middle road, I found that the truth of new and exciting ideas exist in the periphery of our existence. These fresh and interesting concepts are initially obscure and incomplete and it is only through delving deeper by acting without real clarity of the whole picture that your innovation will present to you. This will require trust and belief that you have the capability and talent to acquire the skills necessary to manifest your ideas into action.

When you truly believe that you are a highly powerful creative being, you will create your own form of magic. This opportunity is available for everyone. Have real courage and conviction in your-self and what you are about. You can achieve whatever you set your heart and soul to. It just requires you to take action with what you already know and the rest will present itself to you when you are ready. Allow your-self to dream magnificently and imaginatively, without reservation or restriction. In reaching for the heavens, you are sending your energy in this direction and your loving gift will provide the momentum to sustain you. Know that you have what it takes, do not listen or give any heed to naysayers, surround your-self with encouragement and do not allow your saboteurs or procrastination any power. You have the will to find your way. Be sure always to receive the loving gift of your own creation.

Love—I am infinitely creative in every moment.

CREATE ABUNDANCE

Having an abundant and prosperous attitude is essential to your ability to create freely and joyously in all of your life. In the western world, we have and consume more than we could possibly need in a thousand lifetimes and we still feel like we do not have enough. It is interesting to observe that when you have more than you could ever need, the greater the need to consume seems to be. Do not get me wrong, being successful and wealthy are not to be discouraged nor frowned upon. It is important that your achievements are grounded in the provision of real sustainable benefits to society and represent an equitable exchange of energy for all souls. Just remember that everything is energy and it is essential that we allow energy to flow freely and lovingly for all to share this abundance. The accumulation of energy, the trappings of wealth and hedonistic living can disguise your energetic flow therefore reinforcing and amplifying the very fears and insecurities that may have instigated your initial inspiration and motivation.

When your energy is flowing freely through you from your universal source, you will experience the benefits of this energy within you as you share with others. This is true abundance. When your primary physical needs are met, health, safety, shelter, food and transportation, any further improvement in your standards of living can be considered to be optional. Millions of souls are still struggling for the basics of life while we focus on money, shares, real estate, recessions and the latest electronics. The last time you would have checked, the earth is a closed loop of energy, everything that has ever existed and will ever exist, is still here, circulating and recycling its energy, generation after generation. For such an intelligent and capable species, it is difficult to know when exactly we forgot or changed why we are here and what we are meant to achieve.

You can make a difference and it commences with your intention. When you focus your intention on improving the loving quality of your life, you will feel your connection to quality of all life, regardless of whether it is human, plant or animal. This is when you will know your connection to all life, your inter-dependence and reliance on the whole planet to sustain life and you will know what you need to do to contribute towards the greater good. It does not matter how insignificant you may feel or how small a part you play, it just matters that as you evolve, you pave the way for other souls to find their way. I know that when we know who we are, you will know your role in the evolution of spirit. This is abundance. This is when your energy will flow infinitely and powerfully for as you give to others, you are really only ever really giving to your-self and you will never overdose on universal energy.

Love—I am the abundant source of my creation.

ACTION IS THE KEY

You are a creative being of pure love, light and truth here to manifest your spirit in this physical form. There are many beings incarnation with marvellous and powerful gifts and you are one of them. Every soul has an important role to fulfil. Have you found your role yet? If you have, are you doing all you can with your gifts and have you used your talents to fully understand all of your-self? We create the circumstances and opportunities for our own evolution, acquiring the skills and knowledge to know more about ourselves and how we fit in this world. Every step of your way has led you to your next moment of self discovery and knowing. There are no short cuts or avoiding to this process. We all have to fully experience who we are not in order to find who we really are. When you reflect on your life, you may not acknowledge the courage and faith you have in your-self, however you will clearly see every choice and every significant action has delivered you to this moment of realisation. You have not been standing idle or stagnating. You have grown, understood and learnt more about your existence and this is never wasted.

There will be many times when you question or doubt the sanity of your direction and this is understandable. It requires real effort and conviction to follow your heart's desire, to find the path of your spirit and to sustain your intention when others may mock or deride you. Your relationships will be fully tested and only those tried and trusted real friends will walk this path with you for many souls may not yet be ready. As you set your spiritual intention there is no retreat or exit point, for as you become more conscious you cannot become unconscious or ignorant again. You will not be able to deny your spirit in favour of your old life or old ways. Evolutionary energy flows consistently towards enlightenment. A great teacher once told me that there is no road leading away from spirit, so you will need to be sure of your intention to be your spirit.

As your spirit gains its voice, you will not be able to ignore your own guidance, nor will your soul rest until you have found and acted upon your true spiritual calling. Your guidance, insights and spirit will be irrefutable and grow stronger as you take action with your own wisdom. Learning to listen and act upon your own guidance requires considerable belief and confidence in your-self. Others can show you a way, although you will soon just know to listen to your own voice. If you continue to ignore or dismiss what you know to be true for you, you will find that the flow of your energy will be restricted and grow more challenging. Just let go of needing to know everything, listen to your own whispering guidance and be sure to always take your action with loving intention. It will work out for you. Take action now on the little bits you know, let your energy flow and allow all the vital elements of your dream life to come together.

Love—I act on my guidance with loving intention.

BE LOVE, LIGHT AND TRUTH

You will hear these words iterated in spiritual terminology and possibly pondered their meaning and intention. My simple understanding and experience of love, light and truth as the inspirational energy of my spirit:-

> Love—is pure freedom, free of conditions, unrestricted, unlimited, felt from within.

> Light—is walking your path softly, humbly and lightly, feeling light, free to be.

> Truth—is always being totally honest and loving with your-self and all others.

Love is the primary energetic generator and enabler of the universe. Love is the energy that holds our evolution on its path in spite of all the negativity, fear based, dramatic, painful and traumatic events we create along the way. When you truly feel the freedom of love that emanates from within, you will really know this feeling. If you are feeling trapped, controlled, manipulated, abused, taken for granted, restricted or insecure, you will not be in a loving space. We are conditioned to believe in and seek our soul mates and unconditional love. If you do not feel the greatest, most powerful love of being your own soul mate, you will always be challenged in finding this form of love outside of you. You can only love another as you already love your-self. The love you share runs through you to others. You can never love your-self too much in sharing the abundance of your overflowing love with your loved ones. Your love of your-self shares and receives love from others.

Being enlightened is your full consciousness and awareness of your connection with all energy of the universe. Your soul will be light and free regardless of where you are or what you are doing. This beautiful, liberating sense will prevail in all your life. Your touch, your presence, your demeanour, your whole way of being will become softer and lighter. You will be aware of everything around you, aware of all sounds, colour, sight, fragrances, energy, senses and guidance. You will be aware of your intention, messages and signs and clearly discern your energy field and the energy of others. Living our light is why we are all here. Being the best of our spirit in human form is our collective intention.

Truth is the gift of self knowing and acceptance. To be honest and to act with complete integrity is a desired quality of both our spirit and our humanity. Being true to oneself requires deep self examination, evaluation and acceptance of the positive and negative aspects of ourselves. We are all light and dark, positive and negative, loving and fearful. To accept all elements of ourselves, mastering and transmuting our energy field to be more lovingly positive is our purpose. We have many lifetimes of experiencing our fears in many hideous forms, to reach the realisation that this is not who we are and not how we are meant to live. When you completely know and accept the essence of your spirit in your life, you will know your way and know your truth. Your truth does not require approval, validation or acceptance from anyone else. The only being that needs to believe in you, is your-self and you will be okay with this.

Love—I am Love, Light and Truth.

LOVE FREELY

The purest definition of the feeling of love is to be absolutely free in all your life. Freedom liberates the soul to be all that you are meant to be. Reflect upon those beautiful moments in your life when you felt totally alive, with every cell in your body pulsating with energy and you were aware of everything around you. When you feel free to be all of who you really are, you will find that you are in a pure loving place within your-self and this will be the energy you will share. Until you find this true feeling of love inside of your-self, you will be continually seeking to fill this void from outside of you. This has been our practice for many generations, regurgitated in every lifetime, searching and yearning for fulfilment and love from another when we are not prepared to do the work we need to do within ourselves. Love is pure energy of the heart and soul. If your heart is wounded, protected or closed in any form, you will always be challenged to love and to receive love regardless of how loving you pretend or appear to be.

Who you are is love, pure and simple. Who you have always been is love. Why do we find it so difficult to be this love and to share this love throughout our lives? Generally it is because we have lost our way as a species, believing that we are somehow superior to others, confused as to why we are here and conditioned into separateness and intellectual rationalism. As humans we are quite closed off to the full possibilities and potential of our loving soul's energy. We seem to think that material success is the only measure of a worthwhile, complete life and that we need to compete with and conquer one another in our quest to be our best. This could not be further from the truth. Regardless of your status, wealth, possessions or relationships, if you have not addressed and mastered your spiritual awakening, you will pass onto your next existence by your-self and as unfulfilled as you entered this life. Any unresolved issues, patterns or wounds in your energy field will continue with you through eternity until you take responsibility for healing your soul.

You are the master of your own destiny and it is time for you to free your-self from any energy that is restricting or retarding your spiritual journey. Only you can undo the limitations and old patterns that hold you back from the full expression of your spirit's energy. It still surprises me that we are waiting for something to happen outside of ourselves to provoke and stimulate our changes when the initial spark for this change exists inside each of us. You are the creator of your own life, the liberator of your soul, the master of your own destiny. When you fully accept and embrace full responsibility for the creation of your love for you, you will begin to set your-self free to be all you desire to be. You deserve great happiness, health and contentment in all of your life. Just ask your-self what you need to create to experience these beautiful qualities in your life, set all your intention towards your spiritual evolution and let your energy be free to explore all of your life.

Love—I love freely and openly.

FREE YOUR SELF

You are a free soul of pure light creation right now. Have you found your real feeling of love inside of your-self to set you free? Your love will release you from anything that is holding you back. You may have been conditioned, taught, berated, insulted, hurt or not supported in developing a strong sense of who you are or you were not encouraged to explore the fringes of normality or to take risks to follow your dreams. It does not really matter the reasons why your life is as it is, justification or rationalisation will not provide any answers or improve your situation. Only by changing how you live your life can shift how you are experiencing life and release all the majesty of your own spirit. Every one of us is destined for greatness if we choose to accept this possibility and are prepared to invest the energy into creating our magical life. I do not believe that success is a physical achievement. The real power exists within the divinity of your spirit and when you remember who you really are, you are taking the first baby steps towards setting your-self free.

For far too long, we have given our power away to others including spirit. By this I mean that we give our power away to the Universe, God, Buddha, Mohammed, Ascended Masters, Angels or any other supreme being or energy that we feel is greater than ourselves. We have been conditioned to accept that these external forces provide for us and take away at their pleasure if we do not follow their rules. I know that the universe is a free, loving and ever evolving mass of energy which our souls are all essential elements of. Therefore we are as the universe is, free, loving and ever evolving. There is no separation in this energy field and we are all as powerful as the universe. We are within this infinite energy field, connected, energetic, creative, evolving and all knowing. When you embrace this possibility as your truth, you will set your-self free to fully integrate this energy within your life. Do not be confused with egotistical, insecure power lust; this illusionary energy is not connected to anything other than this transient physical plane.

Choose love as your motivation and intention for all that you create in this life and you will see this love reflected in all that you do. The answer for everything you will ever face will be love. Love liberates, sets you free and releases the full potential of who you really are. When you are in a loving space, your spirit, mind and body will feel free, free of tension, stress and conflict, you will be free to feel clearly and lovingly for your answers and your choices. You are free in this moment. Free to feel, think, express and act upon the essential love that exists within you right now. Feel into how you feel. Let go of any distractions, any fears, doubts or wounds, release any negativity and allow positive love to enter your being and feel the distinct difference in how you feel. Love liberates. Fear restricts. You know the difference, all you have to do is choose love in all of your life and you will be free.

Love—I am lovingly free.

BE VISIBLE

One of the key reasons for you to incarnate in this physical form is for you to be seen and recognised for who you really are. You are spirit in this physicality, striving to be the best you can be, sharing your loving, positive energy with all you meet and living your love through all of your actions. You are a legendary way shower for spirit. For all brave souls who become aware of their purpose, you are not meant to hide or retreat from society. For a time this may be necessary for your inner journey however this is only a temporary transitional period in your journey. Once you begin to remember who you are, you will only be able to fully explore human spirituality by being involved and active within your community. Just as you will not know loving relationships until you are within one, you will not know the complete spiritual condition if you disconnect your-self from others or this physical plane. You are of spirit and you are of this planet. It is therefore important that you involve your-self and your awareness within your community in whatever form you are called upon.

Allow your-self to be visible. Do not hide away or lessen your vibration in order to fit in or to deny your loving intention. When you are within your spirit, you will have the courage and conviction to face all situations, cynics and naysayers. This is your greatest test. Clearing your past wounds and negative experiences will pale in comparison to standing lovingly and truthfully in the public arena. It does not matter what your role may be, it is however important that you show others the way through how honestly and lovingly you share your energy. This is the way of evolution. It requires your spark to ignite the flame of spirit around you and it still may take another thousand lifetimes for us to live fully in our spirit's love, however all transformation starts with your first act of courage. Be brave, be visible and always be true to the love overflowing your heart. You will find your way and be rewarded by developing your own wisdom, courage and faith you will find in your own soul. Believe me you will learn more on the road than you will ever be taught, find in books or be guided to. Your creation of life is magical and mysterious and it is time you enjoyed being free to be you.

Live your life fully in the magnificent glow of your loving light. It will not be possible to disguise or shrink away from your spiritual duty or service. This is not an onerous task imposed by another. You are self anointed and self appointed to your role. That is what is so special about why you are here. You are dreaming and creating your way as you become more aware, discovering the uniquely special and powerful spirit that you are. You are not like any other. You are you and you are required to be all of your-self in all that you do. Sometimes others may not get you or what you are on about. It may take some time for them to catch on, but be sure to have the patience and compassion to share your truth lovingly and softly. It is not that important for anyone else other than you to get what you are about. However it is essential that you do exactly what you have been called to do. Just remember not to ever intentionally harm or hurt your-self or any other soul. When you intend no harm, it is not possible for you to harm.

Love—I am visible in who I am.

LIGHTEN YOUR LIFE

Be the light of your life to find your own way through this and every incarnation. Lighten up in your approach to your life and every one in it, especially your-self. Welcome the light of love in all that you are, you have let go of all your fears, doubts, insecurities and any negativity that exists within your being. As you let go of your human conditioning and programming, you will feel your vibration shift, unleashing any burdens, responsibilities, obligations and load that you have been carrying with you for many lifetimes. The greater the negativity and fear, the heavier the load, the lower you vibrate, the tougher the life you create for your-self. As you release the load of your negative personality, you will become lighter, freer and more loving. The lighter you become, the higher your vibration and the greater the quality of your life will improve and expand. This is self explanatory however we tend to deny that our vibration attracts all other energies into our lives, creating our experience of our life. If we could just accept this truth, we would not purposely make our lives so difficult and challenging for ourselves.

The frequency of your vibration creates your life experiences. You are the creator of your vibration and therefore totally responsible for all you experience, in both the positive and negative sense. If you have had a hard, challenging life, you have created powerfully and negatively. You have infinitely more power to create lovingly and positively should you choose this way. It is just a matter of changing your focus, taking full responsibility of everything that has happened and will ever happen in your life and taking the loving action to improve the quality of your life experiences. When you own your state of being and the life you have created, you have the ability and power to take appropriate action to change it. If you are still holding others responsible or blaming another for who you have become, you will continue to repeat the same experience of your life until you get this truth. No-one else can live or create your life for you, not in any illusion you wish to create, so I would suggest that you do not waste any more energy blaming or projecting.

It is time for you to be the light of your life, to step back into the flow of your spirit and to start being the beautiful loving spirit that you are. You will feel better for it, others will recognise and wonder at your shift in personality and you will begin to really enjoy all of your life. Each lifetime is far too short to be disconnected, fearful, miserable, disappointed and wounded. We pass through this existence so fleetingly; blink and you can miss it. Please do not waste yet another precious life looking for your answers and direction from outside of your-self. You, just as I am, just as all of spirit is, are all the same. We are all inter-connected; all one energy evolving and creating life all around us and it is time for you to play your light being role. So lighten up, free your-self from your own shackles and start living all of your life, you may just enjoy your-self.

Love—I am light and share lightly with love.

BEING ONE

We are all vital elements of the greater soul experience of this physical realm within the body of the universe. There is no separation, no isolation and no external or supreme body that is not connected to you. You exist within the universe; your matter has come from the universe, created of the same energetic elements, all the energy that has ever existed or will exist is within this body. As you evolve, all life within the universe evolves; shifts, creates and expands and this is becoming increasing evident with the changes that are taking place within ourselves, the planet and the entire universe. It is commonly believed that as we evolve, we will become more sophisticated and complex. My feeling is quite the opposite, as you evolve you will become more real, simple and connected. You will not be seeking your answers in technology or intellectualism. You will be more peaceful, aware and compassionate with all life for you will know that this connection is life. You are not meant to disconnect, disengage or waste any precious moment or resource of life. You will know the difference, this I know.

When you fully integrate your spirit and your-self within this wonderful, bountiful planet, you will know you are a soul cell within the greater body of the universe. Just as every cell within your body knows what is going on within you in every moment, every soul in existence has this same ability to connect into everything that is happening within the universe. You have access to all the knowing, all the energy and all the power of every being and every experience through all time and space. This does not mean that you will need to know everything about everything. It means that you have access to the information that you need when you need it. You may access all the information you require or you may just receive glimpses or faint notions. The clarity of your knowing like all things will depend on your own clarity, your own awareness and your own connection with your-self. This is where your-self work comes into being. You can only ever receive the level of information that corresponds with your vibration as you will always be filtering through your own clarity or lack of it. This is also true for anyone you receive guidance or healing from. A good rule of thumb here is to always seek guidance, advice and energy from souls who are clearer and more connected than your-self who will be able to inspire, uplift and enhance your sense of being. If you are still receiving fearful, restrictive or controlling messages, than I would suggest you ask for another opinion, for that one may not be as clear as you would like. Just remember that there is no fear, control, rules, complexity or negativity within spirit, these are purely man-made constructs.

Love—I am a soul within the body of all existence.

LIFE PURPOSE

Are you looking for or have you found your life purpose yet? This is possibly one of the most pressing questions of humanity and is ironically one of the easiest to find when you let go of needing to know exactly what it is. Just as it is with all spiritual truths, everything is opposite to what you might think it should be. Our human programming dictates rational order, sequenced events, linear progress and logical reason. I have found with spirit quite the opposite is true. Everything is dynamic, ever evolving and changing, more simplistic than you can imagine and easier to reach than we have been led to believe. For simple loving beings, we have made our lives far tougher and more complex than they needed to be for both our survival and our evolution. From my perspective, we all have but one purpose and that is to be the best of spirit that we can be in this physical form and that is universal.

When you have little connection to your spiritual nature, you will struggle to find real purpose in life if you insist on living solely through your physicality. Your spirit provides you with your meaning and your sense of real purpose. Physical achievements and acquisitions are purely just physical, temporary and transitory. You do not take anything or anyone with you into your next life. Life and death are great levellers and cleansers of spirit for they ensure that all of us are not only borne equal, we also die equal. Somewhere between these two great points of equity, we have lost our focus. Any being on their death bed with the most toys or possessions, still dies like the rest of us. However the vibration of your consciousness determines the quality of this life, your experience of death and the quality of your next life. Even if this too is an illusion, any investment in your soul will improve the life you are currently living which is always worthwhile.

In accepting our spirituality, you will need to trust that your purpose will present. As you clear your way through your patterns and conditioning, you gain a greater understanding of your-self and you will develop deeper meaning for your life. You will need to trust your inner guidance, to follow your true feelings and have the core strength and belief in your-self to pursue your soul's journey. In walking your truth, you will recognise your signposts showing you the way, piece by piece your awareness will reveal what you need to do next. When you surrender to the flow of your energy, your life will flow beautifully like the pristine stream of energy that you are. You will develop a powerful sense of your-self and you will live your life with real purposeful intent. This is when you will know who you are and you will no longer give your power of creation away at any time to anyone. Being the magnificent being of pure creation that you are will be your purpose and you will always know your way. Trust, commit, love and be your spirit.

Love—I love and live my purpose in all my life.

SEND OUT LOVE

Love is your answer to every question you have ever asked. Love is the pure essence of your life and is the pure energy of your spirit. In our human conditioning we are led to believe that love is something you receive from another, a warm glowing sensation that is stimulated by external means, a place of peaceful contentment when you are with your loved ones. All of this is true, however if you have not found true love of your-self in being able to feel the pure essence of love within and for your-self, you will continually be challenged in receiving love from another. To receive love, you must be the love frequency you desire to attract. The vibration of love that you emit is the vibration of love that you attract. Just as it is with all energies, like attracts like. Your love is your vibration, the greater you love your-self, the greater the love you will create in all of your life. It is that simple and it has nothing to do with appearances, status or possessions. Your love shines from within you, it is real and it is not for sale. Love is as love does.

It is through living your love in all that you do that will show others the way. How you treat, nurture and live your life demonstrates your love. Your clarity of your feelings, how you think, express your-self and physically act upon your wisdom is the only proof of your love that you need to share. You cannot fake your way to love. Pure love is real energy and if you need to pretend to be loving, be honest with your-self and others in what you are doing. Many of us have had to imagine the sensation of love before we have actually realised what it is. If you are still searching for this love of your-self, you cannot take it or receive from another until you are open to this level of love within your-self. Unconditional love is also another fallacy as it is still a condition, therefore it is not free. Also many of us state that we have unconditional love for others, however if we do not have this love for ourselves, we cannot give something to another when we have no idea of what we are trying to give. You must love all of your-self in every way to be able to share your love freely.

You will know when you love you. The experience of love that you feel will be real, liberating and always known within you. It is interesting to consistently find what we have always known has been with us all the time. We have just forgotten, been distracted or disconnected from our true selves for so long, that we have subscribed to believing that we are just our physical experience. Who you are is pure spiritual love. When you fully integrate your spirit within your physical body, you will know your love in a way that you could never receive from anywhere else. Love enables, purifies, heals, cleanses, energises, shares and frees all souls in all ways. When you love your-self, you will not be egotistical or arrogant, you will just be loving. In being all of your love, this will be the energy that you share and your love will disengage you from all negative and fearful projections of others. Send out your love in all that you do, share your love, humbly and freely and always be this pure love of your-self. Love is the energy that powers the light of your soul. Fill your heart with real love for you and others, our glorious planet connected to all the loving energy of the universe. Remember, your heart's love knows no fear.

Love—I am love in all that I am.

NEW REALITY

As you embrace and live the truth of your spirit, you will evolve within the greater reality of universal truth. The world and everyone around will not change overnight, however your view of your world will change dramatically and permanently. You will begin to see more of this life, how we function as physical beings and probably become aware of more dysfunction and negativity than you would care to know. Just remember, that others have not changed, you have and you will need to be mindful of how you share your truth with others. You are now seeing more of what you may have previously closed your eyes to. Be careful not to be too judgemental, critical or intolerant for if you are, you will still be coming from your human programming, not from your spiritual enlightenment. You have been where others are and while you have a role as a way shower, you cannot change or fix anyone other than your-self. Show your way through living the love of your spirit in all that you are. It does not matter if others get you, it just matters that you do.

Your experience of your reality and the universe will be unique to you and it is important for you to ground your energy fully within your body to connect with this wonderful planet. The earth is connected to all existence and it knows its way and its purpose. It is not important that you know all the workings and dimensions of the universe. It is essential that you know all of your-self, know how you connect with the planet and you will be shown what you need to know when you need to know it. As humans we become far too inquisitive and futuristic with our thinking which effectively takes you out of the moment therefore missing the guidance and direction each moment has for you. Spirit is not just another subject for you to master or conquer; it is your experience of your soul's love that is important for you to share.

There is so much energy on this planet for you to experience and share through living the truth of your spirit in all that you do. As you open your energy field to all the physical opportunities for your soul, you will start to experience life in ways that you have previously only imagined. When you let go of your physical limitations, opening your heart to the full potential of your soul connection, you will accept and embrace all the energy of the universe within you. This is why you are here and your fully integrated connection is our collective purpose. Your reality is your creation and as you create the life of your dreams, you will find your reality change and simplify itself beyond your wildest imagination. You deserve to live a full, meaningful and loving life. This is your destiny, all you have to do is take the inspired action required to create this life. This is your creation, set your-self free to paint your own life picture and have the courage to follow your own loving dreams.

Love—I am of the universe in every way.

SOUL'S JOURNEY

Your soul has come from infinity and you are journeying through infinity, so in between there is no need to rush or shortcut this process. Our busy, hectic lives in the quickening pace of time's illusion, dictates that we must do everything in the shortest time, eat fast, love fast, live fast and work hard for most of each physical life. You will know within your-self that this is not sustainable or healthy, for you will inevitably hit the wall that will force you to re-evaluate and change your life style. Unfortunately we seem intent on living our lives the hard way, being all of who we are not before breaking through the facade of our physicality to rediscover that there may be more to life than we have been living. Most people living within this false program cannot comprehend change that they have not experienced for themselves and are often fearful of letting go of their broken life styles even if they are intensely unloved, unhappy, neglected or abused. Each of us has similar stories of discontent and misery. It is only when you begin to awaken your soul's energy that you will realise that there is far more to the life you are destined to live.

Whether you accept the concept of reincarnation or not, your soul is on a journey through time and space, fully connected to all of spirit within the universe and seeking to fulfil its purpose. It does not matter how many lives you have had or what you have experienced in past lives. This information can be useful, however if you concentrate on dealing with what life presents to you in this lifetime, you will have more than enough to deal with, I can assure you. Delving into or dragging up the past in any form will just serve to bring that energy into the present clouding your current situation and creating additional negative energy to clear right now. You are at the pinnacle of your soul's journey and if you focus on dealing with life as it presents, accepting the guidance you receive and take loving action with what you know, you will find your way. Your life will unfold beautifully before you, just do not over think your life, feel for your wisdom in every choice and trust that your soul knows the way even when you do not.

Every experience in every lifetime has led you right to this moment in your awareness and has contributed to your clarity of consciousness. You have had thousands of unique lives in many different forms and you have quite possibly done just about all there is to do and had just about everything done to you. The fact that you are exactly where you are is testimony to the soul work you have done to reach this point in your consciousness. We do not acknowledge the enormous effort and courage required, commending ourselves on the healing we have created and for daring to be different in stepping outside commonly held belief systems. You have come far in your journey, you are beginning to really know and accept all of your-self and you now have the ability to reach further inside of your-self in the universe to really start creating loving magic in all of your life. You are meant to be all of your-self in this place. Be sure that you are fully present, aware and loving in all that you do and your life will unfold beautifully.

Love—I am totally committed and inspired by my evolution.

LIBERATION

Congratulations and commendations on achieving the true freedom of your soul's loving energy. You have endured much and thrived in circumstances where other souls have not dared to venture. For this work, you are highly appreciated and rewarded by all of spirit. Walking the loving truth of your soul on the physical plane is not undertaken without enormous courage and strength of character on all levels. For too long we have given away our power to souls apparently more educated and smarter than ourselves only to find that many of these concepts have disempowered and nullified our innate sense of self. There will be a time when the intellectual and the sensory existences will re-unite and we will become whole again. Every feeling, every thought, every word and every deed is spirit created whether it is actualised with love or not. It is not some omnipresent body that is creating our existence. Each of us creates with every choice, with every energetic act creating the universe in which we live. We will go on creating and recreating life in all its form through all time and space. When we accept our role in this creative process through infinity, you will know how you can best live your spirit fully.

Allow your-self to be completely free in every moment, release any limitations or concepts that limit your soul expression and surrender to the will of your own divinity. Trust that you and your way are okay just the way you are. You do not need to change all of your life, if anything, you may just need to fully embrace the core of you and then follow its desire. Trust is at the heart of your relationship with your-self and all others and provides the platform for you to fill the void of your life purpose. With complete trust in the loving energy of your soul, you will feel absolutely free to fully express all of the liberated spirit that you are. Do not be confused with physical or egotistical expression. You are not your mind, body, status or possessions for these are fleetingly temporary and superficial constructions. Your soul is far greater than your physical life could ever imagine and this greatness is not about physical power, wealth, fame or popularity. Be aware that freedom comes with its price which is absolute responsibility for everything that you create.

Too often we take freedom for granted and abuse our freedoms to fulfil our selfish, ego-centric neediness and this is not freedom, for you are still trapped by your physical insecurities. When you are free, you are liberated and willing to share the bounty of your success with others seeking this same freedom. All souls, all humans have the right to be free, to be living responsible, fulfilling lives in the expression of their spirituality in whatever form that takes. No one has the right to dictate or force their views or beliefs upon others and we all need to respect that we are all unique and we all have our special roles to play. Play your role well my soul friend, we are all in this evolutionary process together and we all share the fruits of our own creation. I know that you know your way; all you have to do is to remember all of who you are and why you are here. Be free and open to all of your soul's love.

Love—I am free, loving and light in all ways.

GATEKEEPER

The keeper of your gateway to all the universe has to offer is always with you. As a conduit of universal energy you have access to all the energy of the universe. You have the ability to determine the energies you work with and utilise to improve the quality of your life. The role of your gatekeeper is to assist you to access the energy you require to accelerate and amplify your spiritual journey and to guard against the energies that do not honour or serve your evolution. Your gatekeepers together with your guides and angels have been with you through this and every lifetime. They know your path, your intention, all of your-self created limitations and they know your destiny. The entire universe has a vested interest in ensuring that we evolve as lovingly and as beautifully as we can to be the best of spirit that we can be. Even when we are forgetful, obstinate or just plain ignorant, they are with you, patiently and lovingly guiding, buffeting and securing you on your intended path. In those moments of your greatest test, they are the feelings, senses or presence that you have felt softly nurturing and guiding you through these ordeals.

Spirit is great abundance in all forms even when we deny, dismiss or doubt the constant loving presence of our own spirit. Remember that spirit is the complete body of energy, it feels, experiences, evolves and loves through all our experiences. There is no separation or disconnection on the spiritual plane even though we may ignore or neglect this connection. Every experience, all life, all events are observed and felt right throughout the universe. Imagine infinity and allow your mind to expand. We all have numerous spirits, guides, angels, teachers, healers, mentors and gatekeepers watching over us all the time. You are never alone and therefore can never be lonely as spirit is within and all around you. You exist in the greater body of all existence. It is time for you to be who you are and to commence creating your life in the image of your own energetic greatness. All of spirit is here to assist and nurture you on this soul journey.

You have the infinite resources of the universe available to you. Allow your-self the time and space to communicate clearly with your gatekeeper, your guides and your angels to let them guide and assist you to find your way. You may let them know your dreams and aspirations, although they already know your path and your destiny. You need to align your-self with their vibration to ensure that you are taking action and clearing your way to the best you can be. Spirit is always with you to enable and support your desires and aspirations. Set your spiritual goals and ensure all your thoughts, words and deeds fully support this intention. The only energy in your way is your own fears and negativity. Deal with your own reservations and limitations and spirit will ensure that you receive all the energy you require. In other words, just let go and get out of your own way.

Love—I am fully supported and guided by spirit.

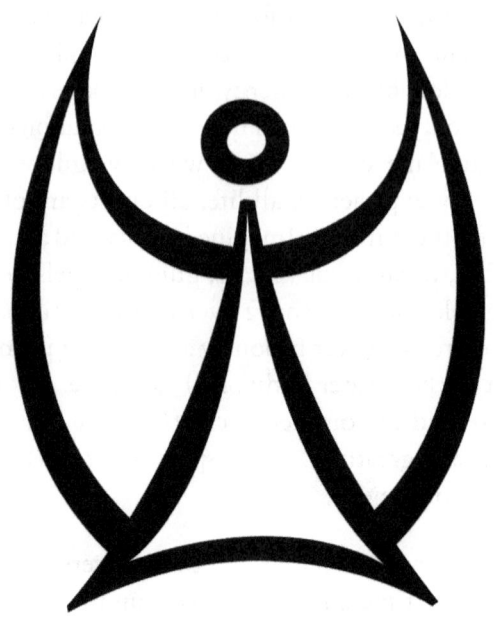

ARCHANGEL MICHAEL

As the angel of strength and courage, Archangel Michael watches over, guides and protects you on your spiritual journey. His energy is infinite and boundless. His role on this earth plane is to ensure all spirits in this physical school of experience receive the resources we need to further our evolution. Remember that you are within the greater body of all existence and when you call on the angels, your guides or any spirit, you are really only calling on this aspect of your-self. Yes, all the energy of the universe comes from within you, not from some external source. You are the source of all your experiences and this includes your experience of your spirituality. While this concept may be contrary to your programming and be challenging for you to accept, this has been my experience. All of us have access to the universe through our access to our own spirit. When you can accept this possibility, you will see all of life and its illusionary construction very clearly. Connect with your spirit and you will connect with all spirit's energy, past, present and future.

Archangel Michael is within you, just as all the angels, masters, guides and great teachers are. You are connected to all forms of life and you share the experiences of all spirit within your spiritual body even if you still struggle to accept this reality. When you feel the presence of spirit, you will feel this energy within you. For those of you who channel other spirits you will feel their energy within you, connecting, morphing and merging with your own energy field, expressing and amplifying yet another aspect of your-self. We all have the ability to access spirit, just place your intellectual self aside, stay out of your way, quieten the mind and let the pure loving energy of spirit emerge. It is unfortunate that most of us only reach out to our spirit when we are tested, down or challenged. It is far easier to access spirit when you are in a clear and loving space within your-self. You will be attuned and resonate with spirit's energy, enabling you to clearly and easily hear their messages. At first you may only receive flashes, hints, glimpses or single faint words or whispers. Listen quietly for the pure loving intention in these messages. When you act upon this guidance, you will receive and hear more of your universal gifts.

Angels are messengers of the supreme beings, they oversee, guide and nurture you on your journey ensuring that you always succeed and prosper. They cannot intervene when you are determined to learn the hard or painful way no more than you cannot obviate the learning or healing of another. All change is your creative responsibility, all growth is your growth and all healing is your healing. When you access the angels, you will tune into an energy field greater than your own and you will not be the same again. Be aware of your aspirations and dreams for you will create with these intentions. Michael will provide all you ask for, just be sure of your requests for you will create your desires. You have all the power of the universe within you, just be your-self and you will know this to be true for you.

Love—I connect, listen and act upon Archangel Michael's guidance.

ARCHANGEL RAPHAEL

Archangel Raphael is the angel of your loving heart guiding you back to your love centre. As the angel of the heart, Raphael communicates in clear loving language enabling you to feel real love for you at the very heart of your being. You will feel the truth of his loving pure intention liberate your soul. Allow your-self to open up to really feel again, to be vulnerable and sensitive to all the energy of the universe emanating from your powerful love centre. Raphael will amplify your love; you're immense feeling of love and create the space for you to explore all of your love. There will still be times when you forget and struggle with old patterns and conditioning. All you need to remember is to call on your love energy for your answers and guidance and listen to your love. It is important when you are releasing any negative or fearful energy to take the time necessary to clear and heal this energy with loving kindness nurturing your soul. You cannot avoid or circumvent this process no more than you can force water through sedimentary rock to create clear, pristine ground water. Your spiritual journey is a similar process, your patterns, conditioning, programming and behaviours need to be gently and lovingly sifted and cleansed through the time that it takes. Any attempt to circumvent this process will just recreate the same experiences for you to face all over again, possibly in an amplified form.

When you come from the loving space of who you are, you will know each step of your way and you will have access to all the guidance that you need. You will know the difference between the messages that love and honour your journey and the advice that constricts you with fear and negativity of who you were not. Spirit through you and others always communicates clearly, simply and directly with pure love and positivity in all ways. You will know when spirit is within you based on the loving truth that you feel. Listen to this loving guidance, feel the truth for you, take from each message what you need right now and take action with what feels right for you. This is all that is required of you, no more, no less. You are the master and creator of your own destiny and only you fully experience all of your own choices. Be sure to act with loving wisdom and your path will run true. The angels provide guidance and clarity; however they cannot live and love your journey for you. Only you have the power to change the quality of your life. Be sure to create from your loving centre and this love will flourish in all of your life. Love can only generate and encourage love.

Love—Archangel Raphael guides me with love and kindness.

ARCHANGEL GABRIELLE

Archangel Gabrielle, the angel of mercy, love and compassion is here to guide you. Gabrielle can show you the way home to your spirit. Let go of all judgement, intolerance, cruelty, anger, doubt, insecurity, fear, hurt, pain, regret and any negativity that resists or sabotages your spirit's love. You have created and experienced great hardship and trauma to create your awareness. You have observed your enormous power of creation through your own negative, fearful attraction of drama, deceit and suffering in your life. This energy illustrates your ability to create negatively and fearfully if you do not choose another way for your-self. You have infinitely greater capability and power to create with pure love and positivity as your intention for all that you do. All you have to do is to come back to your spiritual essence and commence creating with loving, positive intent in all that you are. Your seeds of intention create your life harvest.

Gabrielle will show the way to your compassionate, merciful self for you. You do not need to fight, compete, struggle, strive, quest, conquer or stress at any time. Let go of these debilitating behaviours and beliefs and set your-self free to fully experience real love. Your love will clear your way. Sometimes you may find your-self in situations you have experienced previously, try not to judge or criticise your-self. Bring the situation into your awareness, observe clearly how you created your issues and seek the loving answer to whatever you are facing. As you evolve you will continually face similar circumstances to see them from another perspective and to clear them fully from your energy field. Healing is similar to weeding a garden, you may pull out the obvious weeds, however if you do not dispose of them effectively or leave any seeds behind, you may find some issues may regerminate. The more you tend and nurture the garden that is your soul, the easier and simpler this cleansing process becomes.

Allow the energy of spirit to run through you to be all of who you desire to be. The angels are very powerful and effective in enabling your energy field to set itself free of human conditioning and negativity. You are meant to be totally love and truly positive. All you have to do is to allow your spirit to be lovingly free to express itself and to commune with all the energy of the universe.

Love—Archangel Gabrielle enables my spiritual growth.

ARCHANGEL URIEL

As the angel of your spiritual connection, Archangel Uriel plays a key role in activating your true spiritual nature. You are so close to having a real sense of who you are, closer than you may acknowledge and live in your everyday life. Uriel is with you, guiding and teaching you to express all of your-self in every moment. Showing you another way to be, teaching alternative beliefs and concepts, providing insights into unique knowledge of age old practices, adapting and modifying the way you experience your world. Through Uriel, you will find the original path you intended to forge your spirit's energy. You are here to be all of your-self, in your form with your own gifts to share with the planet. You are finding your way, listening and understanding that all of your life is here to teach you more about who you are.

By integrating your spirit into your life, you have listened to Uriel's guidance whether you are aware of these insights or not. You will continue to be shown your way through all your senses and your feelings in every moment. Listen and act upon your guidance and you will find your-self in places beyond your wildest dreams. You cannot intellectualise or plan your way to the power of spirit. Thinking we have all the answers is one of the most common shortcomings of human judgement. Spirit has a great sense of humour with this age old cosmic joke, "How do you get God to laugh?—You tell him your plans". While you are busy planning and thinking, life goes on, growing, shifting, evolving at an ever quickening pace in forms unrecognisable or comparable with the past. If you continually address your issues with the same solutions that created the problems in the first place, you will just repeat your learning. We need to find new, more loving and enabling methods of addressing the human condition and we need to be more inclusive in resolving human suffering, poverty and isolation.

This is where your life is important. You have a key role to play once you have achieved greater awareness of who you are and why you are here. You are meant to act upon what you know to be true to assist your-self and other souls. You are part of the whole, a vital element of spiritual expression and you have significant energy and love to share with and assist others. All you have to do is let go of any remnant, redundant and miniscule fears that are holding you back and allow your-self to express the full love, light and truth of who you are. You have come a long way to reach this realisation, do not miss or waste another opportunity to make your difference in sharing your love and positivity. Now is your time to shine.

Love—Archangel Uriel connects me with my spirit.

NEW BEGINNING

In the past, the spiritual journey has been overly complicated, controlled, secretive and mystified throughout history by numerous scholars, preachers and inquisitors and I am certain that many of us have been involved in this process. I do remember many lifetimes where I have been in positions of immense power and privilege, working with energies far more powerful than these symbols and creating many concepts that we are still living by today. As you study and observe history, you will see that little has changed, we have just become more sophisticated in how we live and die and seemingly less civilised in how we connect with each other. I know that my previous life in this body reflected this disconnected intellectual existence. It can be quite challenging to live the truth of who you are in the general mainstream, surrounded and bombarded by mass living and stimuli. This is not to say that it is impossible, it just requires the soul to develop more loving and honouring processes to remain whole and conscious of any compromises or sacrifices you are making. Where you find your-self will always be perfect for your evolution. You will need to be more aware of your guidance and to listen intently for your loving truth amongst all the distractions, noise, busyness and intellectual chatter.

Being able to live the truth of your spirit is the greatest gift you can ever create for your-self. The insights, energy and information you attract into your life will guide you back to your true self. Everything will not necessarily ring totally true for you; it is for you to discern for your-self what you are prepared to try and to make the choices that honour your soul's journey. Do not give your power away to me or anyone else for we are not responsible for your choices, you are. You are the only soul who is creating and living your own dream life. If you have family, you are also responsible for how you honour and respect your family unit. Ensure that you do not intentionally inflict any harm upon your-self or anyone else. You are the creator of your own energetic destiny. Always create with pure loving intention for this will determine the quality and frequency of your vibration, your karma and your lives.

How you feel within the core of your soul is the catalyst for everything that you create, energetically and physically. Your feelings will always be pure, loving, simple and honouring for your-self. When these feelings come into your mind you will process, translate, compare, interpret and analyse to create your thoughts. Depending on your consciousness, your thoughts will be either positive and loving or fearful and negative. This focus will determine whether you are in a responsive loving mode or reactionary emotive space. Herein lies your loving or fearful choices. Feel into your core feelings in every situation you create and you will observe that the initial feeling can be similar regardless of whether your mental interpretation is loving or not. When you are either excited or nervous, notice your initial feeling will feel similar until you start to think. It is your thoughts that attach their meaning to your experiences. How you think, respond or react will determine the words you use to express your-self and generally these words will reflect your state of consciousness or lack of awareness. How you think and talk about others will always express your insecurities and fears projected upon others in an attempt to make you feel better. Your words are powerful and they can empower and inspire or they can disable and hurt. Be mindful of how positively or negatively you release your energy to either enhance or hinder your spiritual journey. As you express will be how you create and act in your reality therefore creating your experience of life. If life is working out as you desire, than you are consistent in your intention and on track. However if you are continually creating conflict, discord, hurt, pain and suffering in your life, maybe it is time for you to take responsibility for this creation and for changing your ways. Unless of course this is all you believe that you deserve out of this life. As you feel, think, express and act is how you release your energy to create the quality of your life karma. This energy will be energised by the level of joy or pain you feel in the creation of this karma and so too your life will be until you take the loving action to make positive changes.

Listen to all your guidance regardless of where it comes from or who shares it with you. The most unlikely of teachers will present just at the right moment to give you a nudge, share some wisdom, present a new insight or just say the right thing at the right time to provide another piece to your spiritual jigsaw. Take everything in, receive all your guidance graciously and take action with what feels right to you. Let go of needing to be totally self reliant and independent, you do not always need to know everything or have all your own answers, you are allowed to find an easier, more loving way to your soul. This is really what this work is all about. These symbols activate, release, energise and stimulate your journey, enabling you to find yet another key to your puzzle. You are allowed to take in everything that works for you, learn from the experiences of others, read the signs in everything you encounter without over analysing or critiquing every little thing. All signs have meaning, although some are more important than others to follow. Be sure to know the difference and to be able to accept each piece of guidance immediately in its time for that too will pass quickly and you would have missed your next piece of guidance.

Life is for living and loving and be sure to create an abundance of both, preferably together. You have the soul right to live a beautiful, magical and whole life, full of loving freedom, great health, happiness and prosperity. Be open to all of your-self, to all of spirit and share your energy freely and lovingly in all that you are and in all that you do. You deserve to live the very best of lives and you will achieve greatness in your life when you fully accept and believe in all of your-self. This has been my experience and I am honoured to be able to share my love with you. This has been the journey of my life and I feel blessed to know more of my loving self. I live for the day when billions of souls have evolved with total awareness of their loving spirit and we have all mastered living with real love in all of our lives. That is my dream.

Create your own dream for your life. You have the power and creativity to imagine an existence far greater than you are currently experiencing. We are all connected in spirit and I pray you have received what you have needed to accelerate your loving evolution. Allow your wings to unfurl and open broadly to all the magical possibilities of life. You know your way and you know who you really are. Open your heart, connect with your mind and live your loving truth in all of your life. In every moment you are forever changed and guided towards your destiny. Your life has begun, beautifully, magnificently, abundantly and freely. Just be you.

ABOUT THE AUTHOR

Ken Dowling is a powerful spiritual channel, sculptor and teacher who has consciously been on his spiritual journey for the last 14 years. He came to his spiritual realisations after 25 years hard labour in the corporate world, cumulating as an Executive Manager with a Masters in Business Administration (MBA) and managing over 2500 people. Late in 1997, he had a premonition that if he did not change the way he was living, he would have less than a decade left on the planet and within six months his whole life imploded. His marriage of 17 years ended, he lost his career, his family and friends, most of his material possessions and he completely transformed every aspect of his life. Over the next three years, he investigated, explored and discovered many different belief systems, philosophies and insights into how he could live with greater love, contentment and purpose. Prompted through this journey of self-discovery, he found most of his answers inside him-self; he has listened and applied his own unique perspective and wisdom to his spiritual gifts. He believes each soul is unique with its special gift to share.

His journey really started when he inscribed Usui Reiki Symbols on his Universal PowerPole sculptures where he was led to the creation of these Universal Symbols. He has now created over 10,000 sculptures sharing this special energy right around the world. These sculptures are energised and transmute all negativity and fear to create the flow of positive, loving energy in their environments. There are many stories from satisfied customers testifying to the benefits they have received from his work. Ken's real skill lies in his ability to simply communicate his message in a very loving and practical way. He shares his love freely with everyone who invites his guidance and he empowers everyone to find their unique way to their spirit. He has adapted, re-invented and created his own spiritual methodology that enables people to change their lives at a pace that suits their personal style. He is in tune with his senses, is highly sensitive to energetic resonance and dysfunction and strives to live his truth in all of his life.

Ken also operates a spiritual clinic on the Sunshine Coast, Australia where he offers healings, teaching and counselling on a personal or group basis. He is a regular feature at spiritual festivals and markets, openly sharing and guiding souls looking for a different spiritual way. He has touched thousands of souls, challenging and transforming their perspective and contribution to life. Ken has the ability to feel what is happening within the soul body and provides practical remedies that assist to resolve physical and spiritual discord. Everyone who has felt his energy is forever changed for the better. He is a special soul who lives his love with purpose. When you allow your-self to really feel, you will know how you need to live and this is when you will receive his universal gift. He just asks that you follow your heart's desire, set yourself free to be all of who you can be and walk softly with your love of life as your inspiration and guide. Love truly is the light of your soul.

INDEX OF SYMBOLS

Abundance and Prosperity 154
Accept to Forgive 68
Action is the Key 212
Answers to Life 84
Archangel Gabrielle 242
Archangel Michael 238
Archangel Raphael 240
Archangel Uriel 244
Attract Loving, Positive Energy 150
Awaken Your Consciousness 36
Be Discerning 82
Be in Each Moment 32
Be Love, Light and Truth 214
Be Visible 220
Being One 224
Blessings 190
Bring Your Self Together 194
Choices of Life 202
Clarity of Sight 182
Cleanse Your Aura 116
Clearing Patterns 90
Clearing Negative Energy 70
Compassion 50
Courage 174
Create Abundance 210
Create in Every Moment 180
Creativity 208
Crest of Change 200
Deserve the Best 152
Detachment 128
Embrace Change 196
Embrace Your Gifts 144
Embrace Your Life 142
Enlightened Journey of the Soul 170
Faith in Your Self 104
Find the Joy in your Heart 176

Flow of Positive Energy 40
Flow with Life 164
Focus on your Self 34
Focused Intention 80
Free Your Self 218
Fun and Joy 44
Gatekeeper 236
Grace and Harmony 138
Gratitude 140
Higher Self 78
Holy Trinity 192
Honour and Humility 186
I am Spirit 30
Intuition 72
Journey into Completeness 168
Journey Within 48
Just Be 42
Learning Focus 60
Let Go of Resistance 88
Let Life Be 160
Liberation 234
Life Purpose 226
Life's Lessons 64
Light Protection 120
Lighten Your Life 222
Love and Truth Guide You 166
Love Companion 178
Love Freely 216
Loving Relationships 62
Motivation 172
New Reality 230
Open your Heart 52
Opening to Opportunities 204
Ownership and Responsibility 132
Patience 184
Peace, Balance and Harmony 136

Quieten the Mind 58
Receiving Heart 54
Relax 156
Release All Pain 66
Release Anger 86
Release Your Potential 112
Remove Energetic Hooks 114
Remove Protection 118
Repelling Negative, Fearful Energy 148
Sacredness 188
Seal Your Aura 122
See the Beauty Within 98
Self Belief 96
Self Confidence 110
Self Love 100
Self Reliance 126
Self Responsibility 56
Self Value 106
Self Worth 102
Send Out Love 228
Sense of Purpose 198
Serenity 162
Severing Karmic Links 92
Shifting Consciousness 38
Simplicity 46
Soul Expression 130
Soul's Journey 232
Spiritual Focus and Discipline 134
Stand Tall in Your Power 124
Surrender 158
Take Back Your Power 94
Trust in Self 108
Trust Your Truth 76
Universal Energy 206
Walk Your Path 146
Wisdom 74

www.ingramcontent.com/pod-product-compliance
Lightning Source LLC
Chambersburg PA
CBHW070638160426
43194CB00009B/1497